For Kathleen

through me & that's
great! ☺

/Jacob
Samuel '17

For my family.

 Cartoons on pages 40, 61, 87, 111, and 177 first published in *The New Yorker*. Cartoons on pages 64, 100, 155, 172, and 207 first published in *Prospect*. Cartoons on pages 13, and 171 first published in *Money and Family Law*.

All other cartoons first published at *thedailysnooze.com*.

First edition: May 2017

Published in Canada by Nap Burrito Books

SLINKY HELL

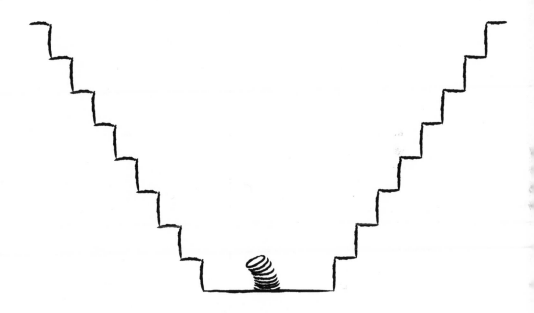

and other cartoons by

Jacob Samuel

Nap Burrito Books

Animals

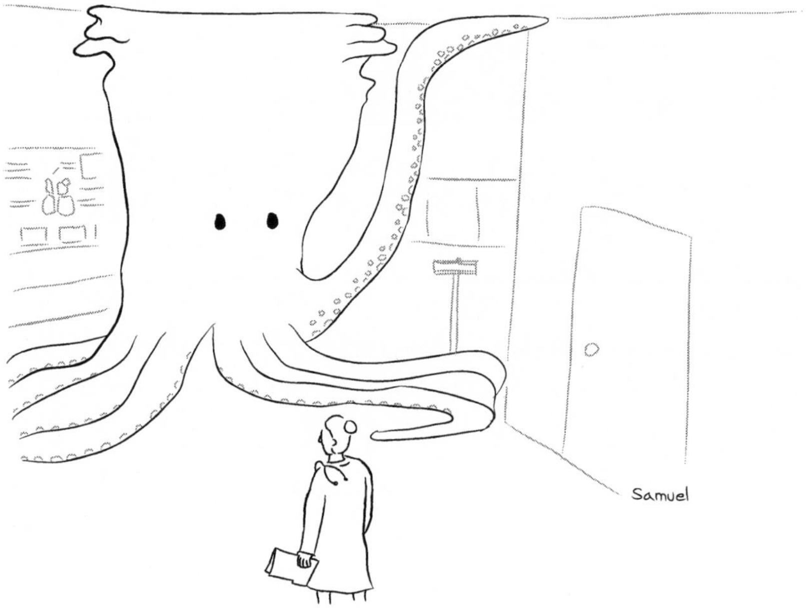
Samuel

"I'd like to see you cut back to eating only two, three ships a day."

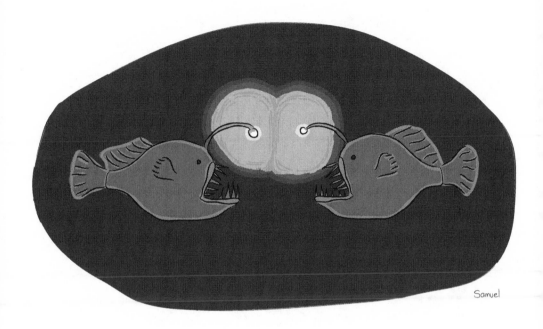

"Just once I'd like to be attractive
not for my pulsating light, but for my personality."

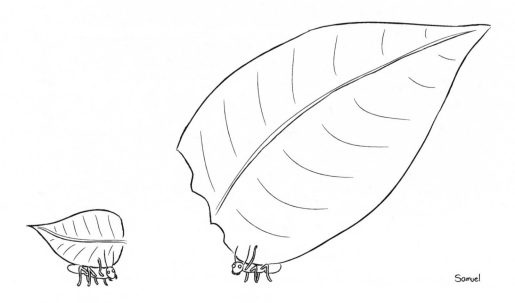

"I thought we agreed to pack light."

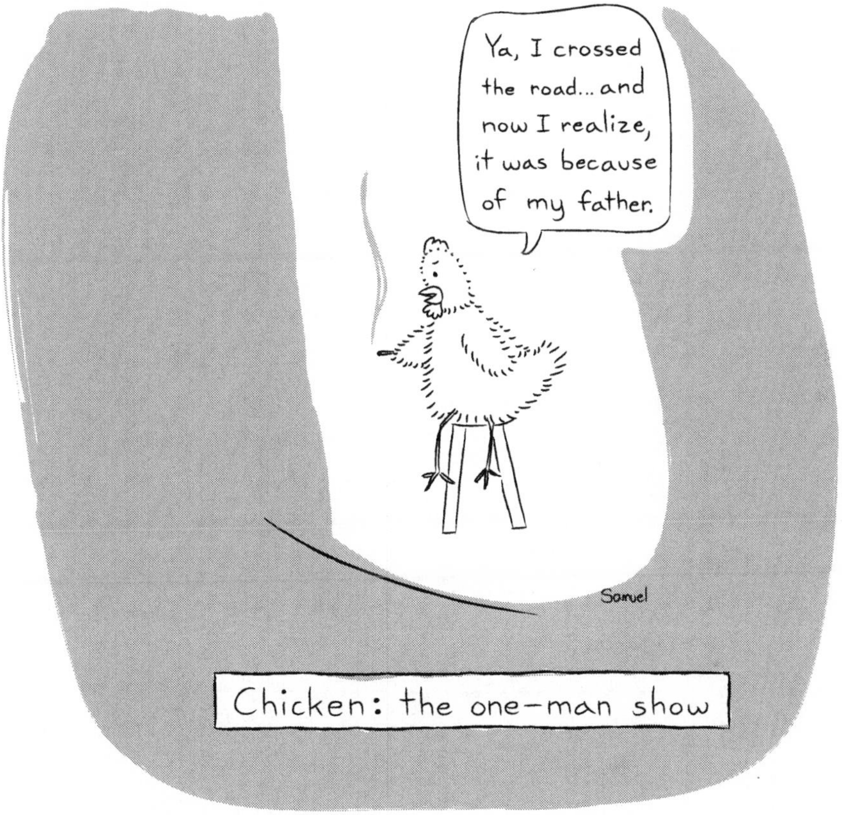
Ya, I crossed the road... and now I realize, it was because of my father.
Samuel

Chicken: the one-man show

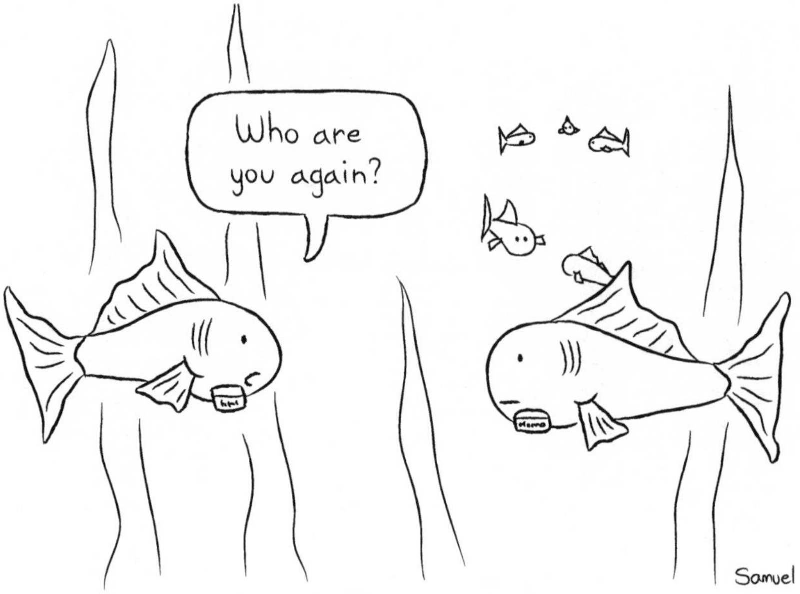
Who are you again?
Samuel

Goldfish four-second reunion

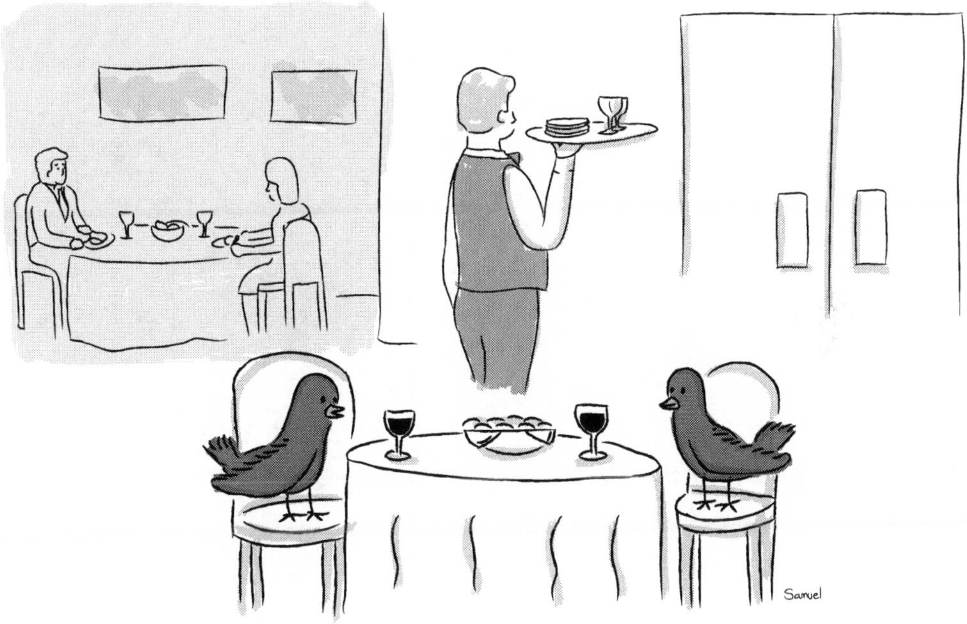
Samuel

"This time, let's not just fill up on bread."

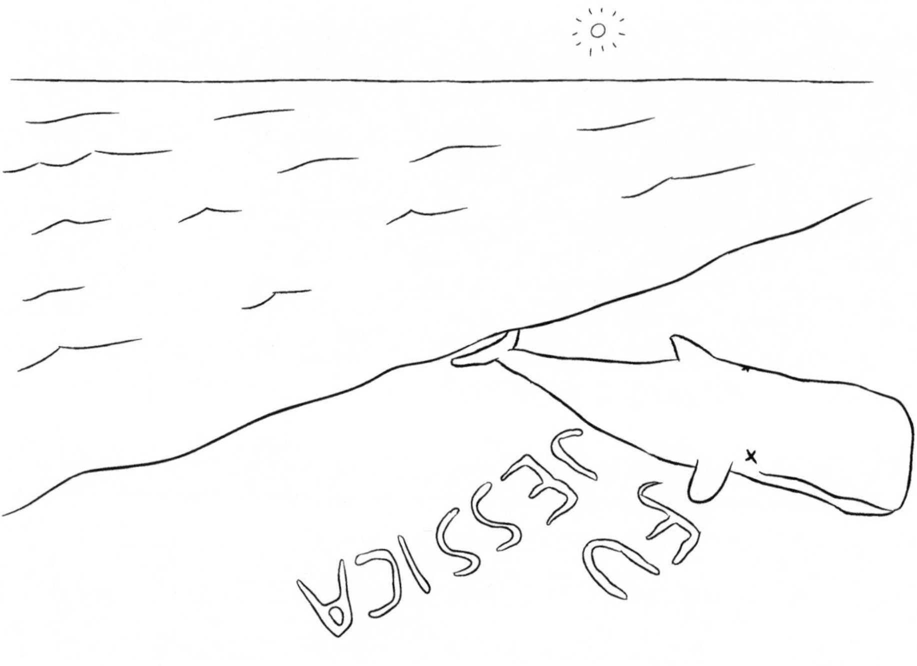
JESSICA

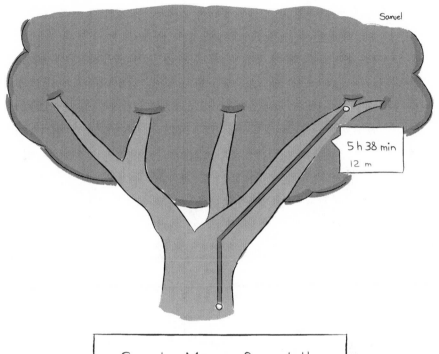

Samuel

5 h 38 min
12 m

Google Maps for sloths

9

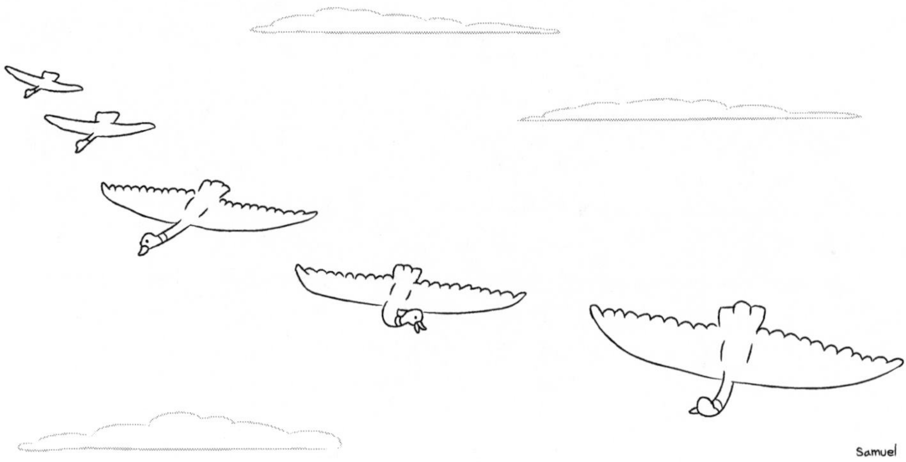
Samuel

"Next year, let's fly on points."

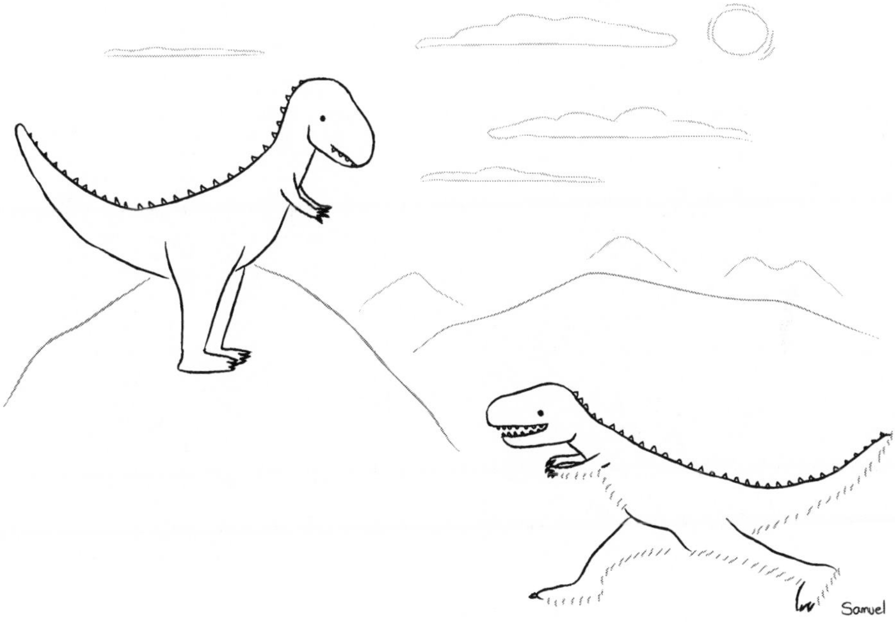
Samuel

"What about now: would this look good as a fossil?"

Samuel

"Show off."

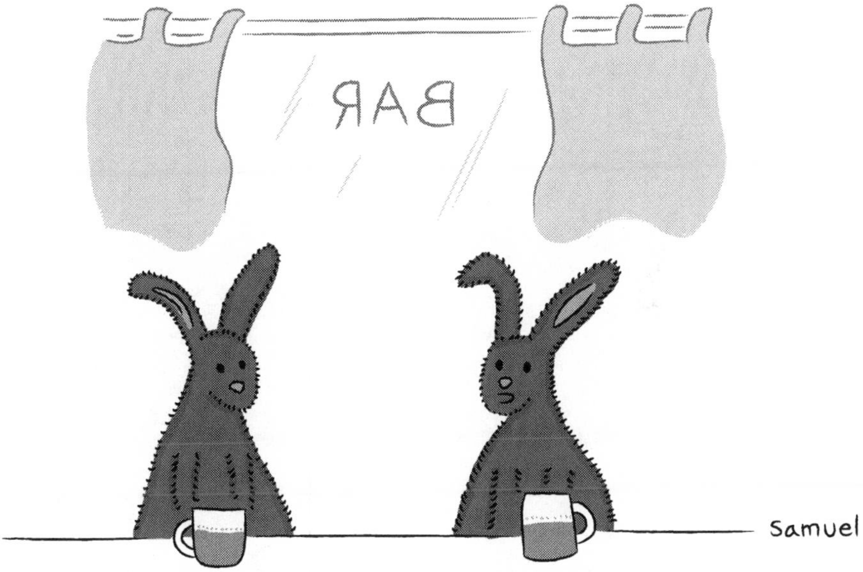
BAR
samuel

"The divorce is fine, but I'm getting killed on child support."

Samuel

"Sell it."

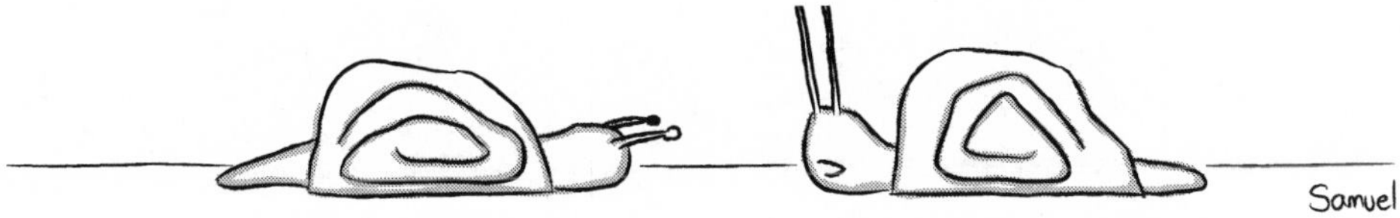
Samuel

"Hey! My eyes are up here."

SELF-
ACTUALIZED
ESTEEMED
LOVED
LOVED
LOVED
SAFE
SAFE
SAFE
SAFE
SAFE
Samuel

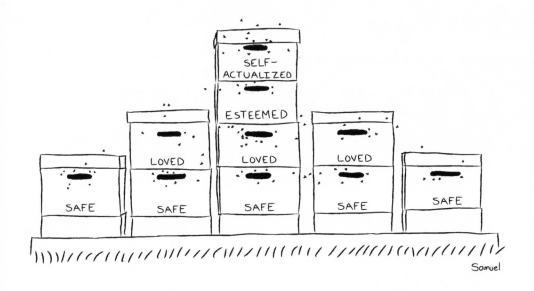

Maslow's hierarchy of bees

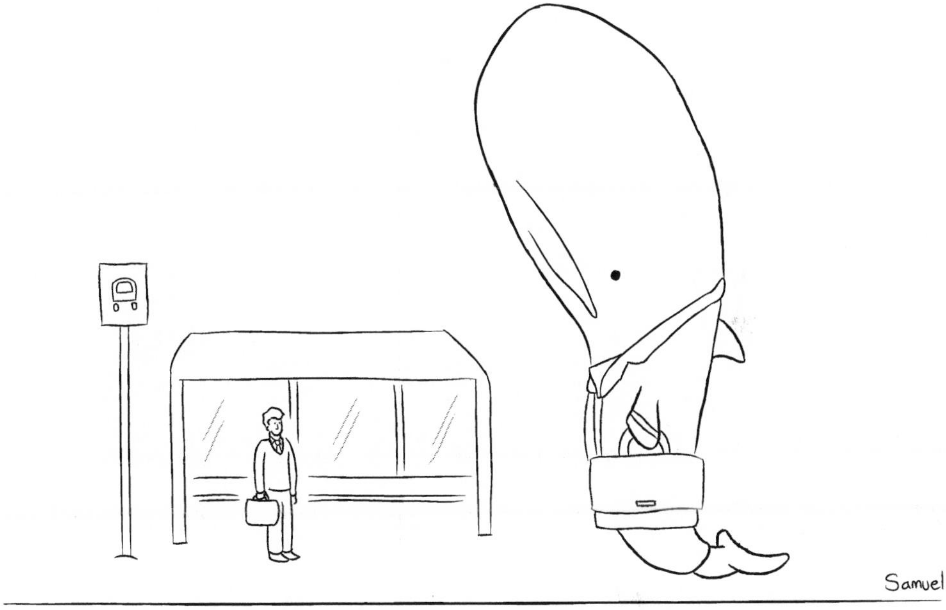
Samuel

"I'm thinking about going to the beach later."

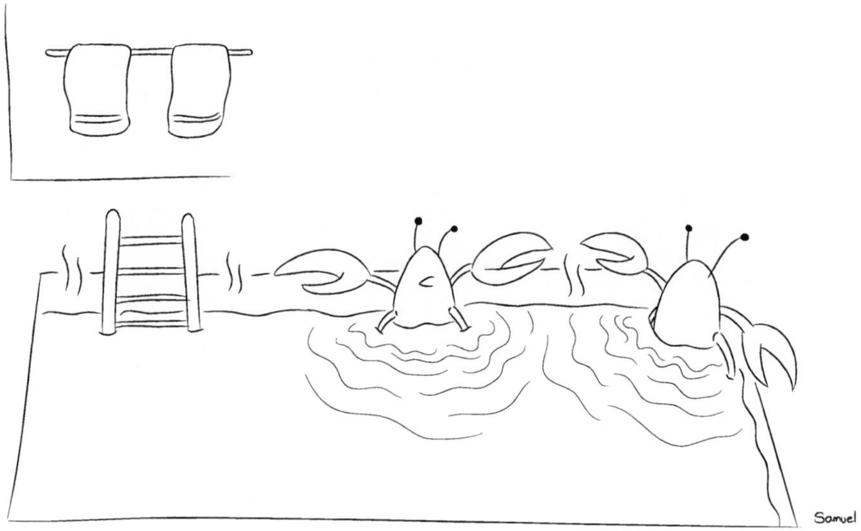
Samuel

"Frank, you're starting to turn red. Frank? Frank!"

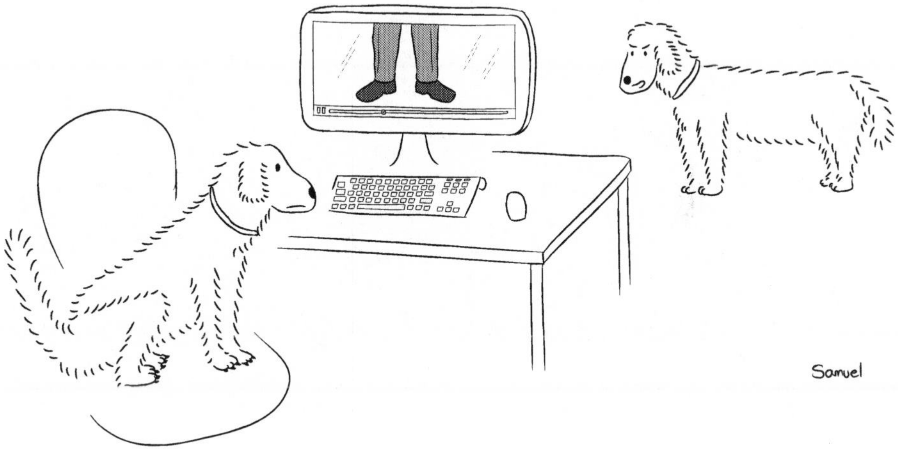
Samuel

"Are you watching porn?"

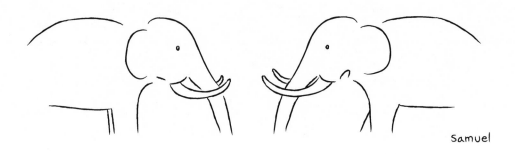

Samuel

"I can't stop thinking about the Alamo."

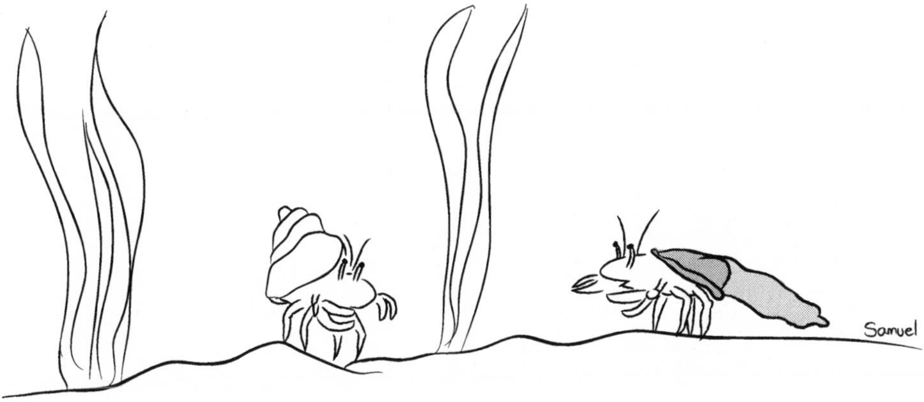
Samuel

"The housing market crashed."

Samuel

"<u>You</u> try staying this thin
after giving birth two million times."

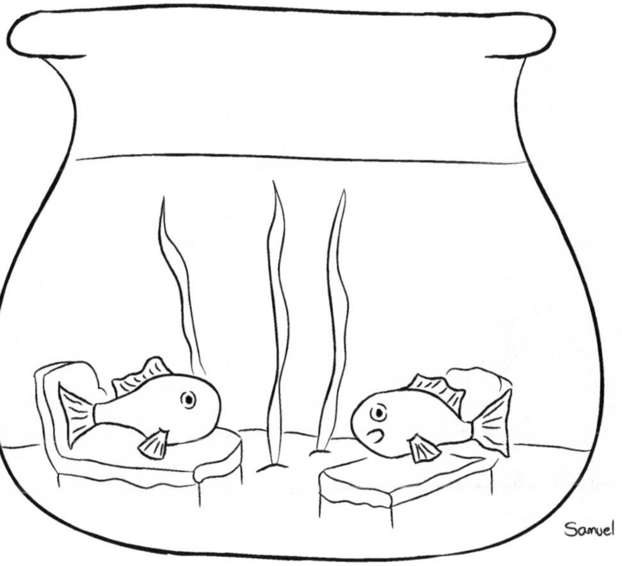
Samuel

"I forget which one of us is the therapist."

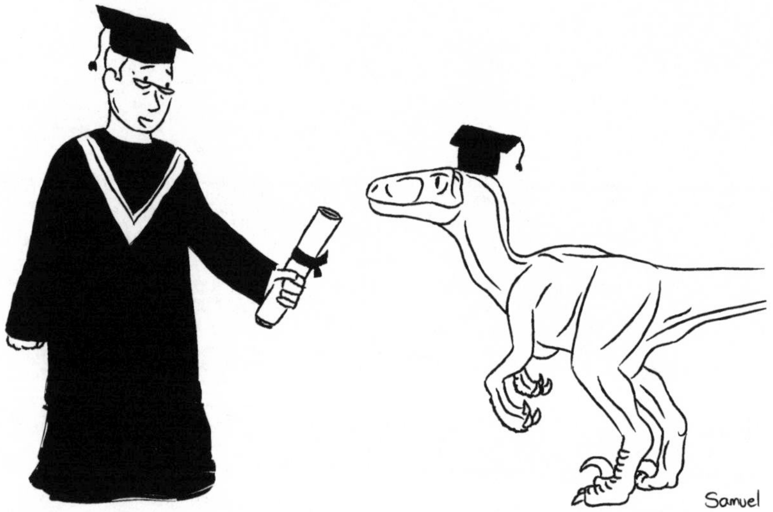
Samuel

"Clever girl."

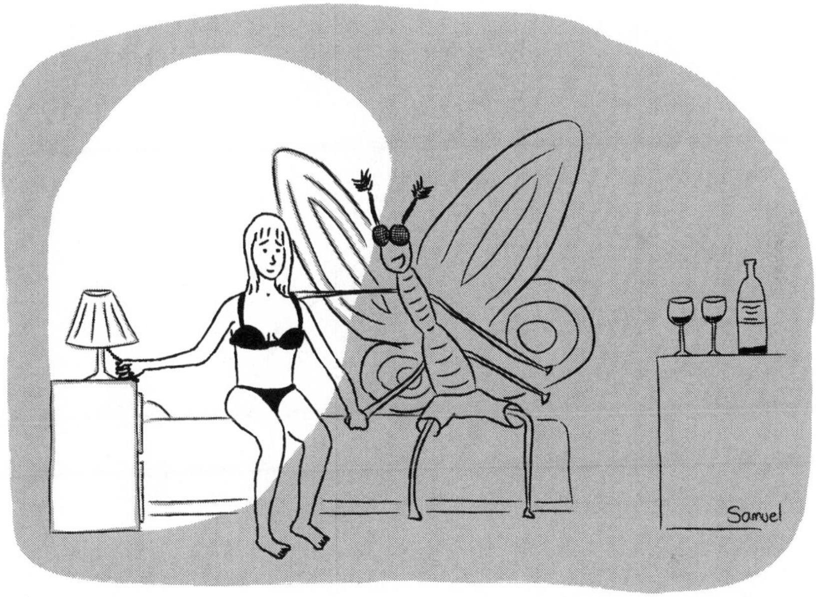
Samuel

"Wait—leave it on."

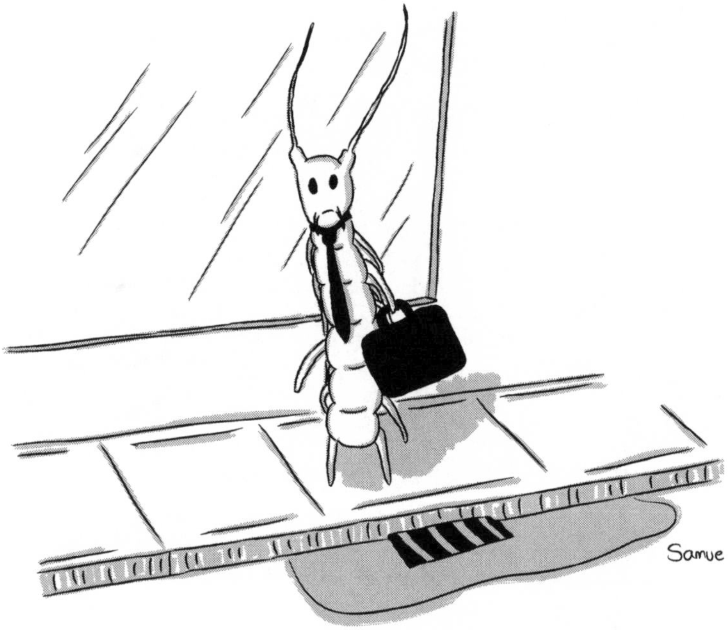
Samue

THE OTHER HUMAN CENTIPEDE

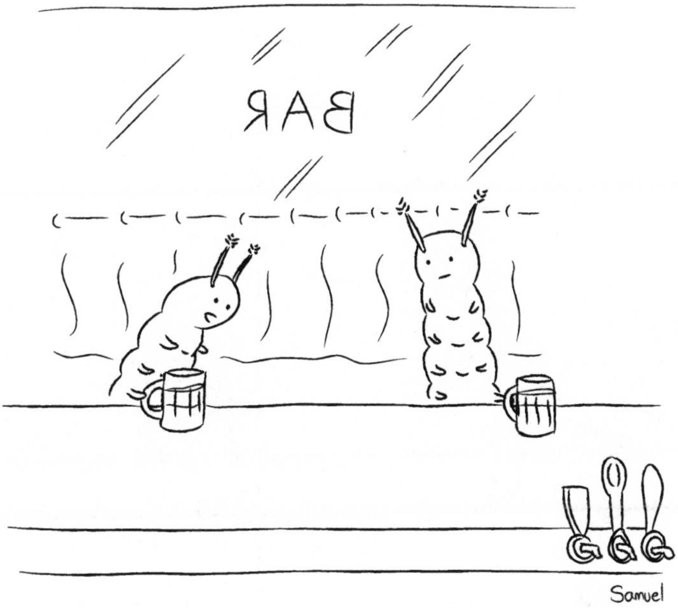
BAR
Samuel

"I found out I'll never turn into a butterfly. I'm a moth."

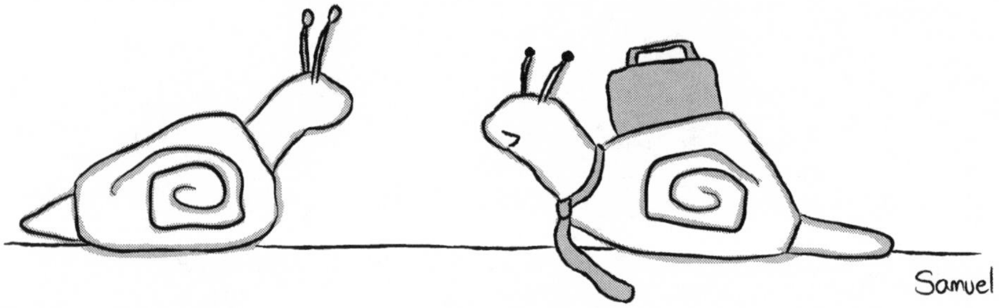
Samuel

"My survival strategy is negotiation."

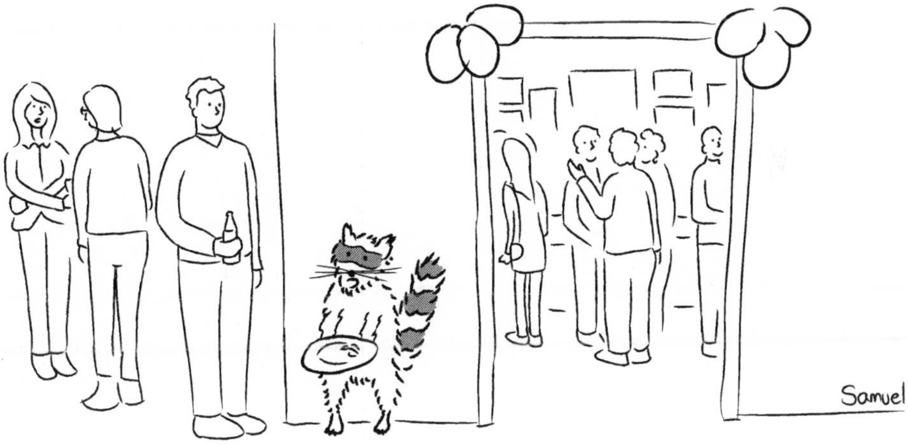
Samuel

"Where's your garbage?"

Samuel

"The weight doesn't show
if you only eat other snakes."

Death

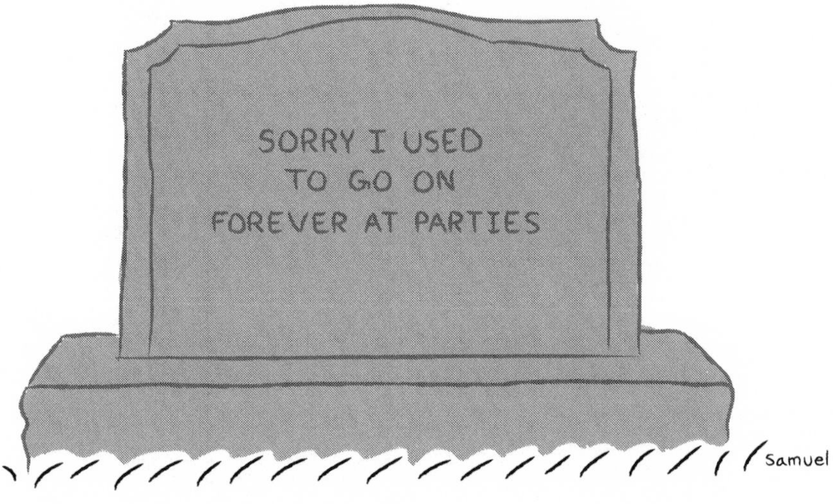
SORRY I USED
TO GO ON
FOREVER AT PARTIES
Samuel

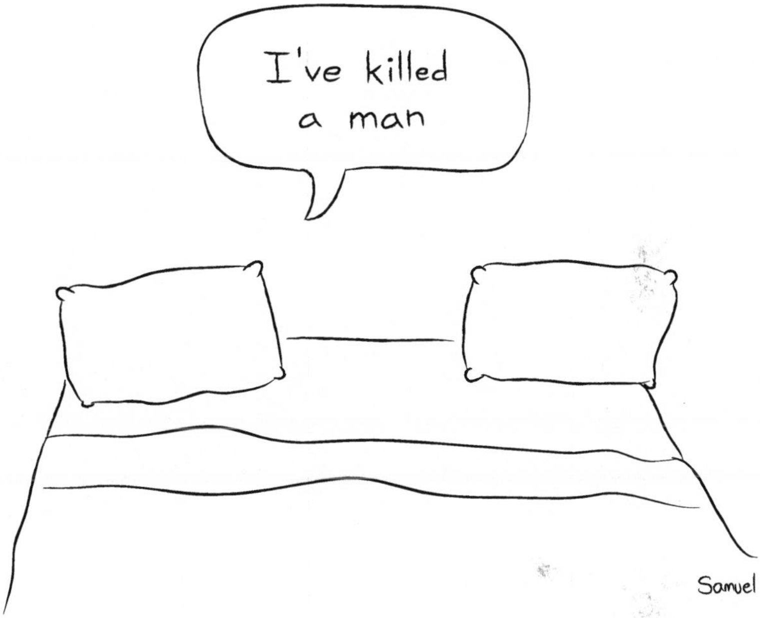
I've killed a man
Samuel

Pillow talk gets real

Samuel

Samuel

"They had a groupon."

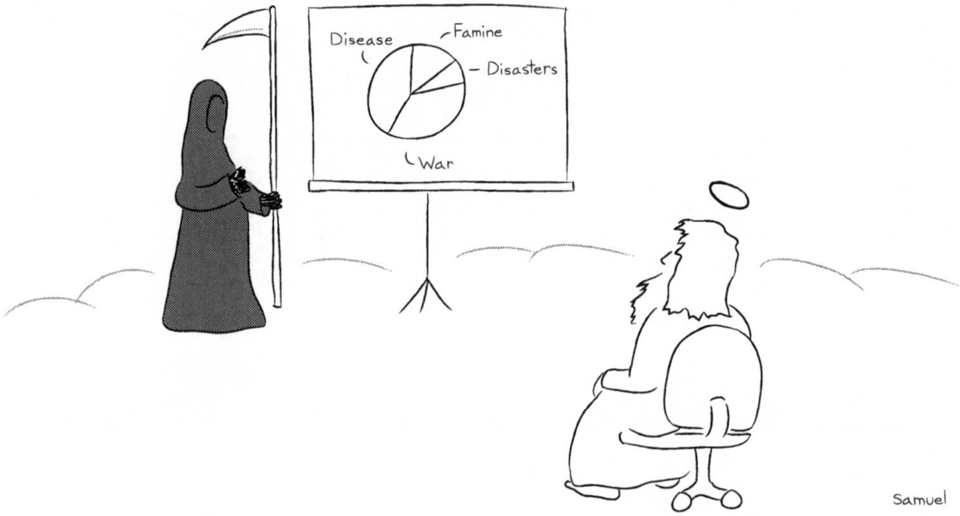
Disease
Famine
Disasters
War
samuel

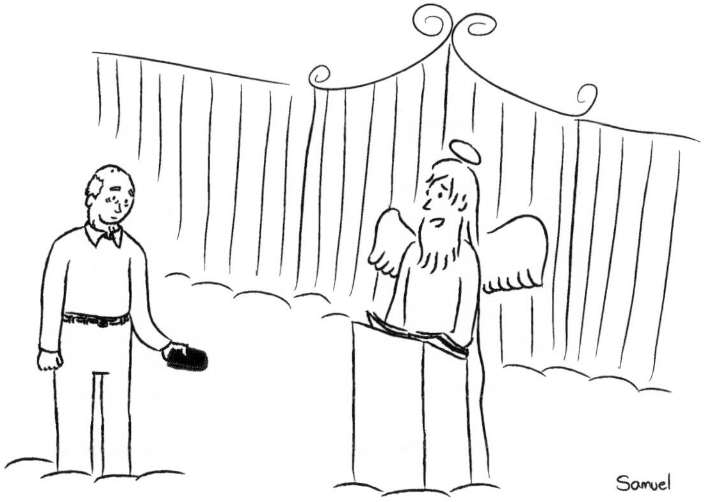
Samuel

"Now you should get a text message from us for two-step verification."

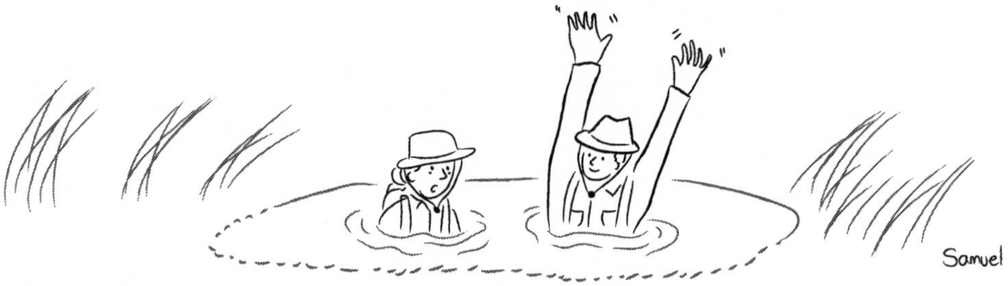
Samuel

"Carl, now is not a good time for jazz hands."

Entertainment

"Planet of the Apes" in French

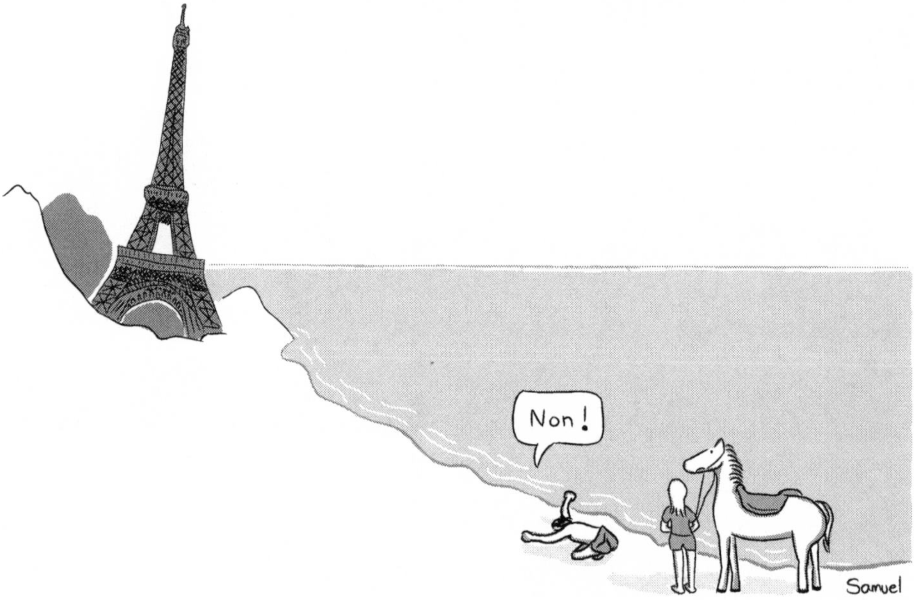
Non!
Samuel

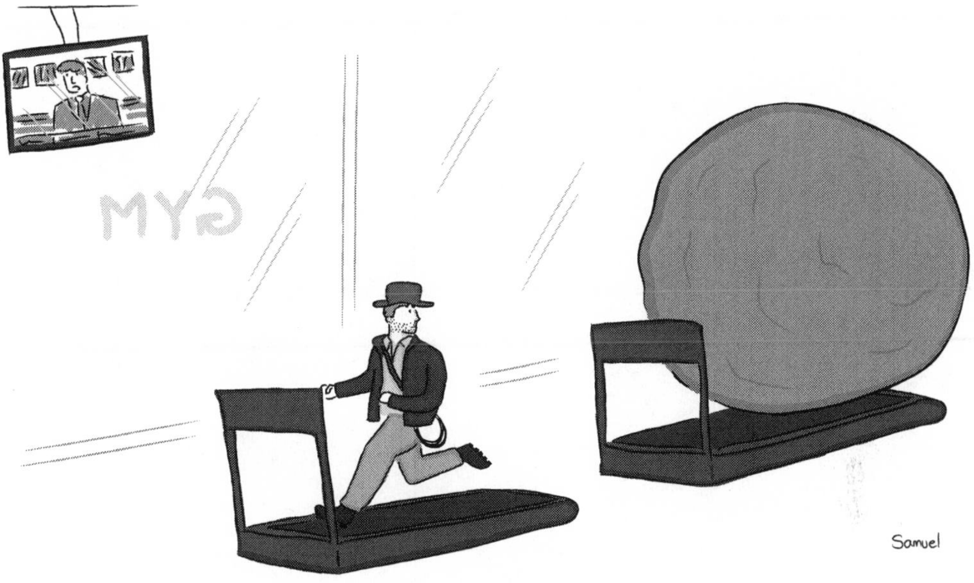
GYM
Samuel

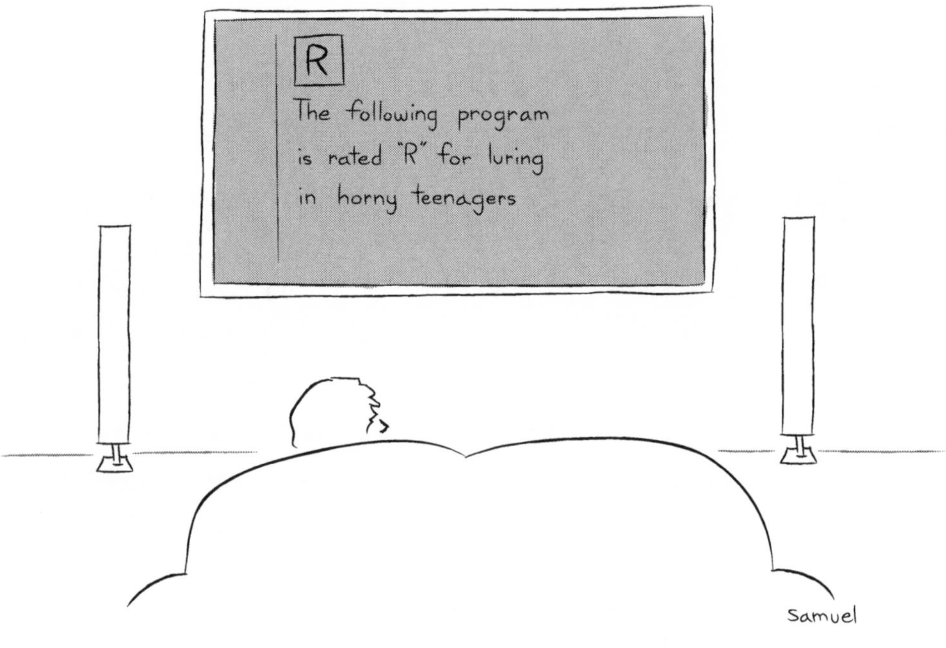
R
The following program
is rated "R" for luring
in horny teenagers
samuel

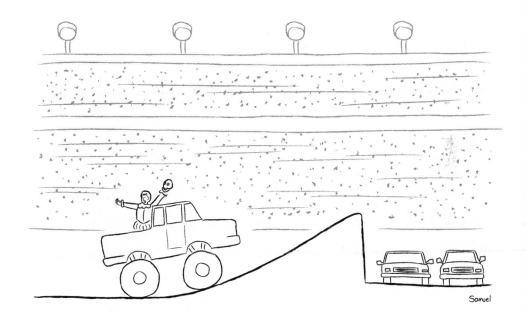

Shakespeare in the Thunderdome

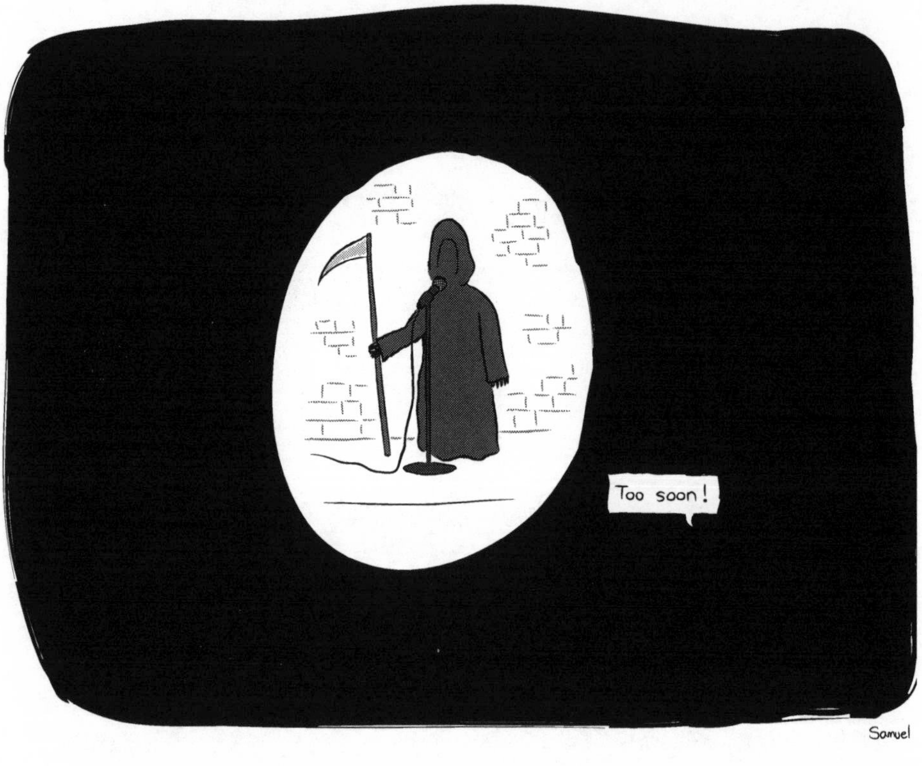
Too soon!
Samuel

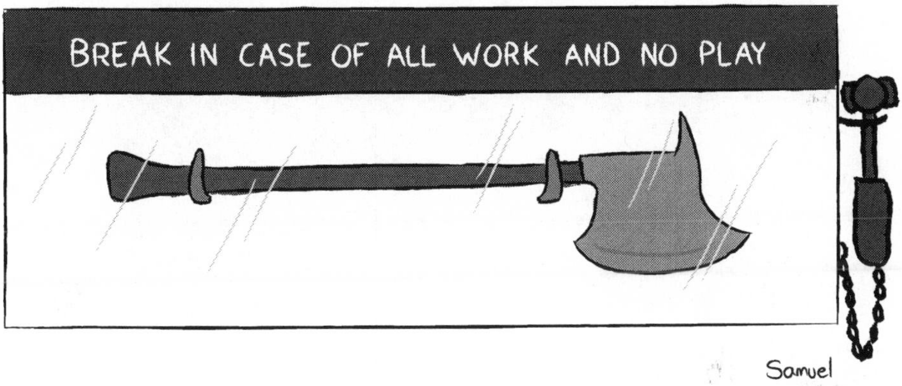
BREAK IN CASE OF ALL WORK AND NO PLAY
Samuel

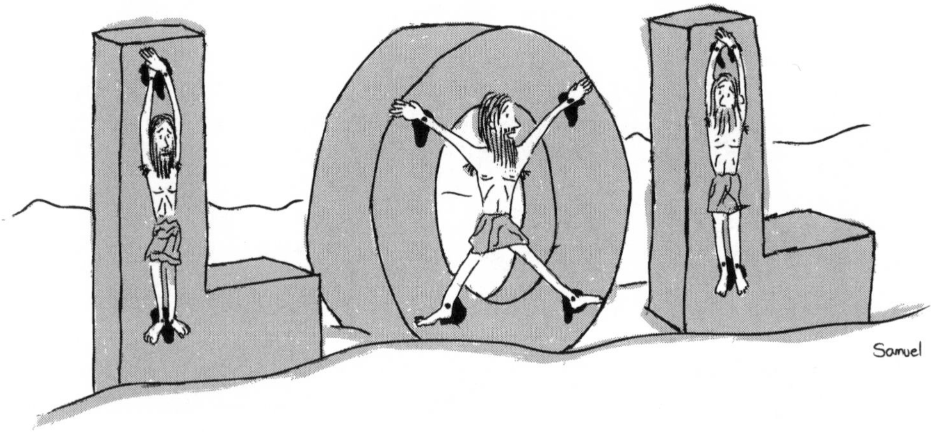
Samuel

"This is the most I've ever felt like a real comedian."

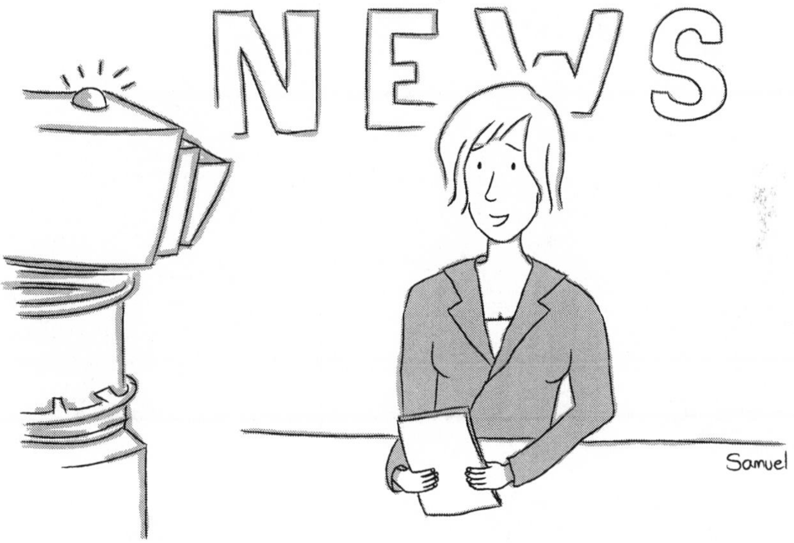
NEWS
Samuel

"In today's news: I'm attractive."

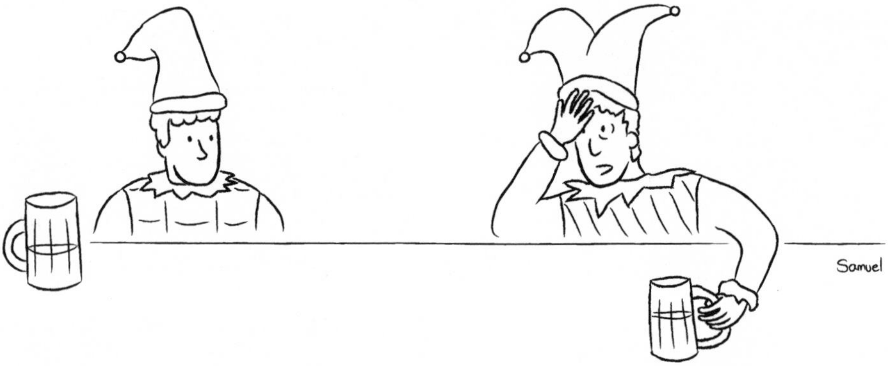
Samuel

"Sometimes success just leads to a chance to fail in front of more people."

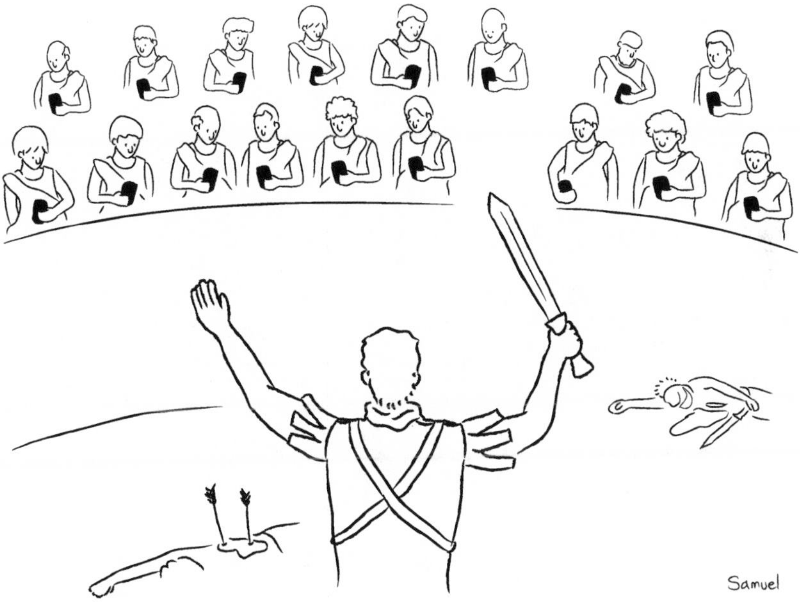
Samuel

"ARE YOU NOT ENTERTAINED?!"

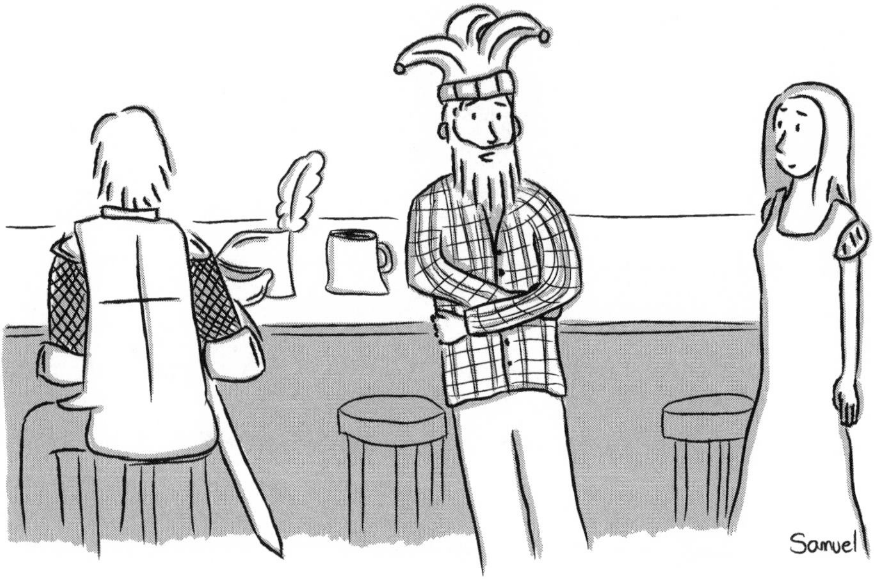
Samuel

"The kind of jestering I do is more 'alternative.'"

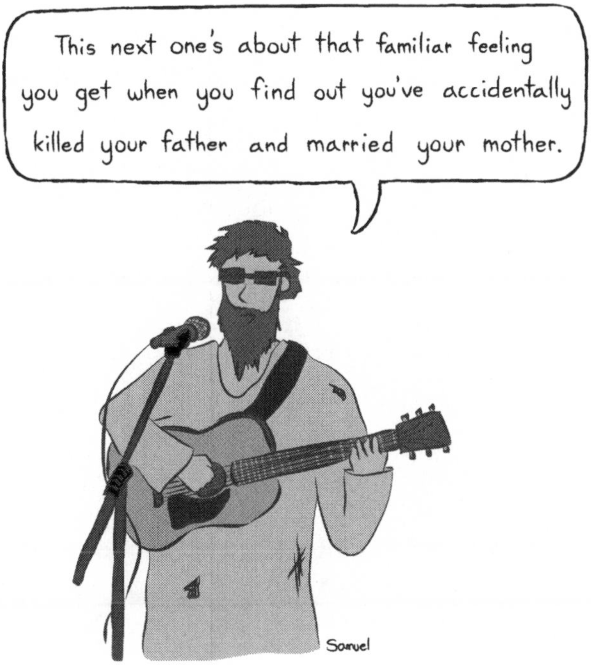
This next one's about that familiar feeling you get when you find out you've accidentally killed your father and married your mother.
Samuel

OEDIPUS HITS THE OPEN MICS

Samuel

"Not tonight."

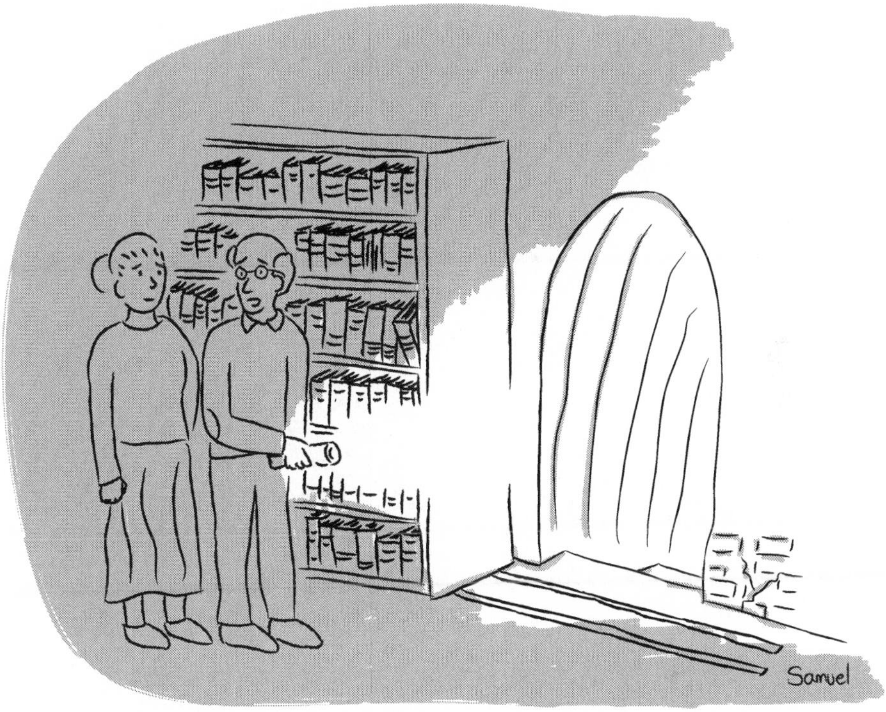
Samuel

"I hope it leads to more books."

Hipster Casablanca

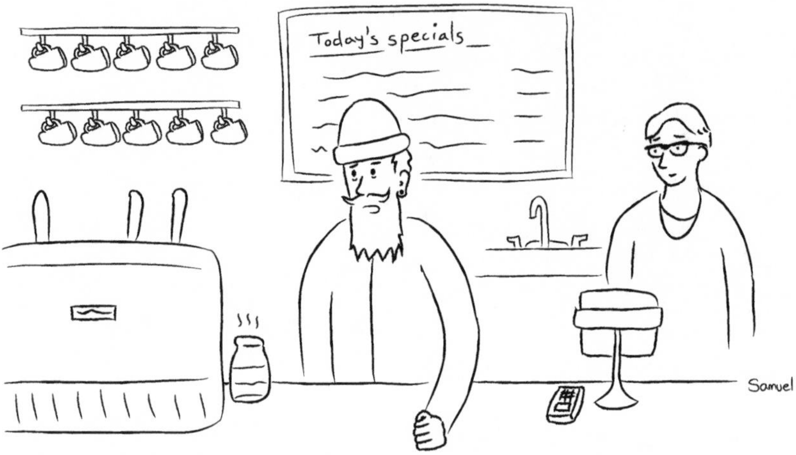
Today's specials
Samuel

"Of all the fair trade, vegan friendly cafés in this gentrifying post-industrial neighborhood—she had to walk into mine."

Family

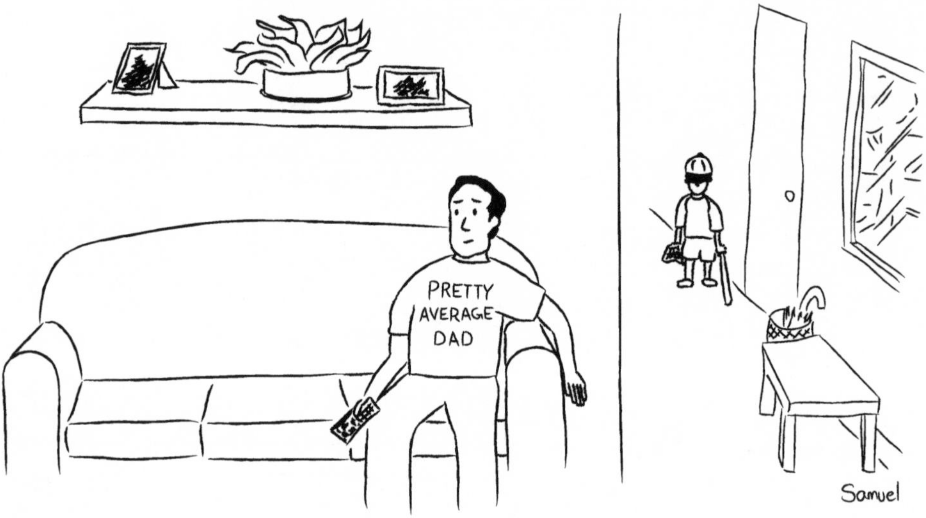
PRETTY
AVERAGE
DAD
Samuel

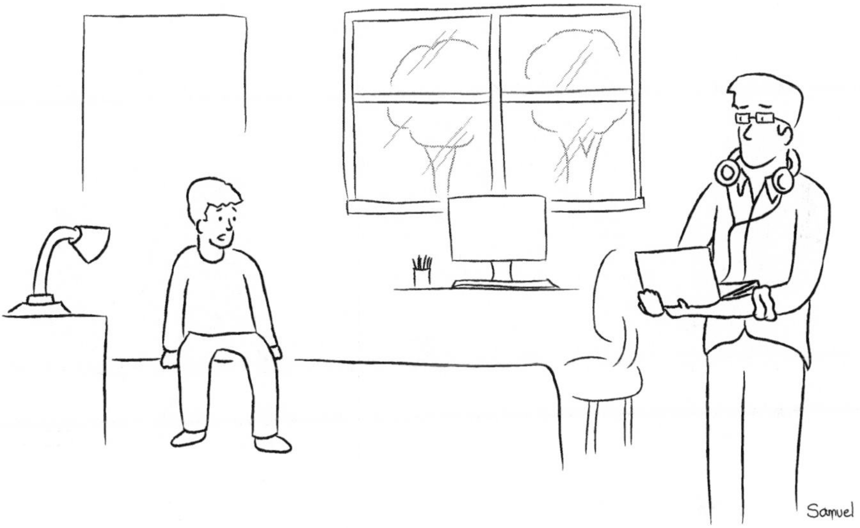
Samuel

"Dad, can I talk to you not on your podcast?"

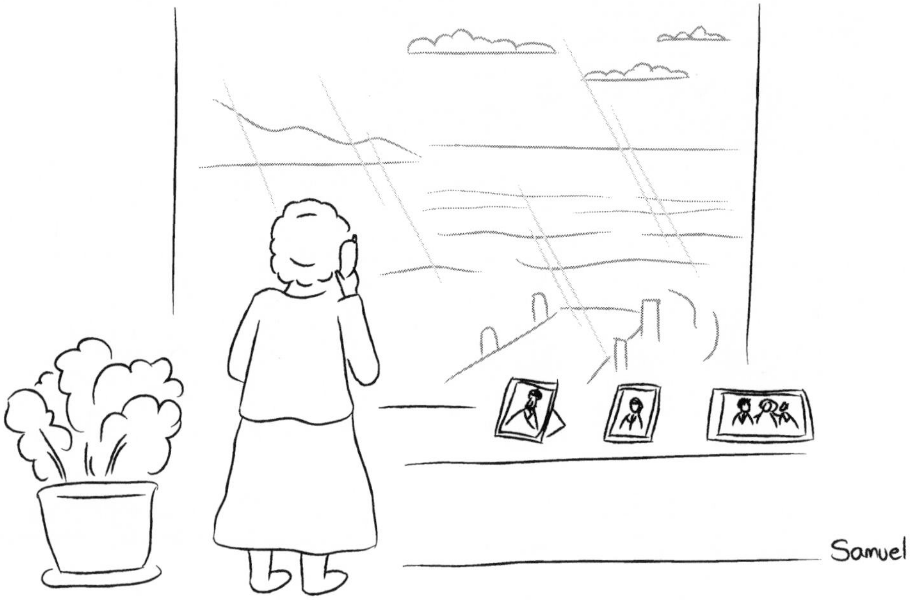
Samuel

"Call me, Ishmael. It's your mother."

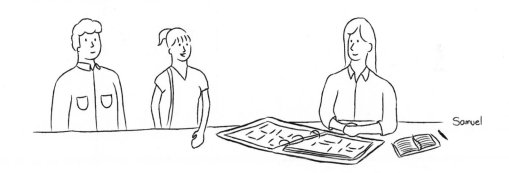

Samuel

"We want the theme of our
wedding to be 'rich parents.'"

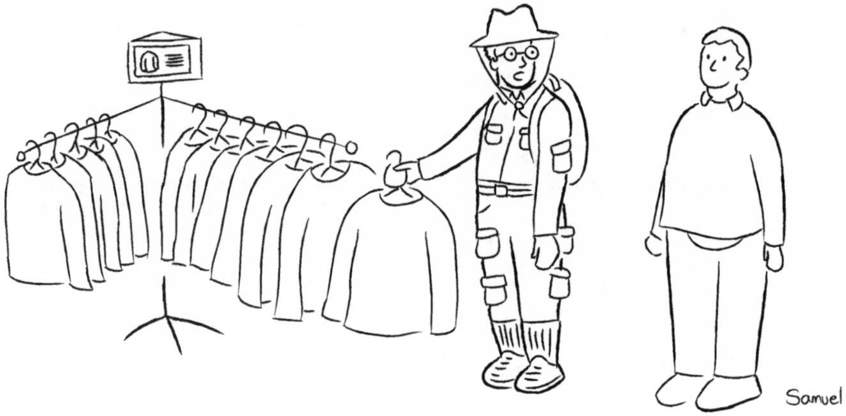
Samuel

"Now that I'm retired, I've started dressing like the rest of my life will just be one long hike."

Samuel

Take Your Work to Daughter Day

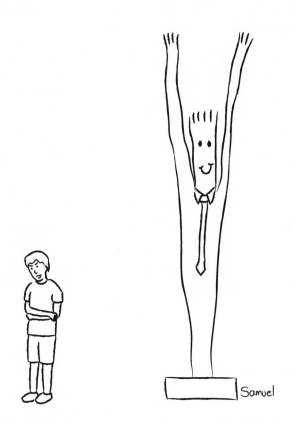

"You're not even my real dad."

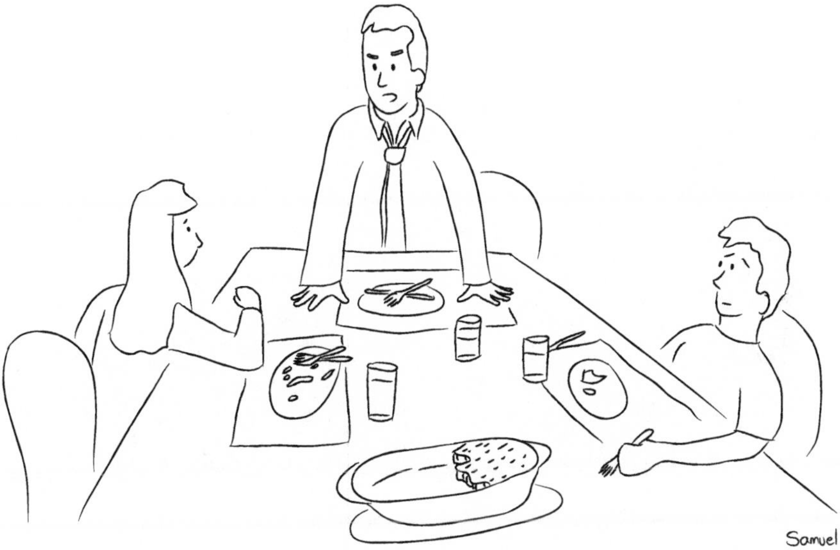
Samuel

"You'll be excused once I'm done instilling you with my politics."

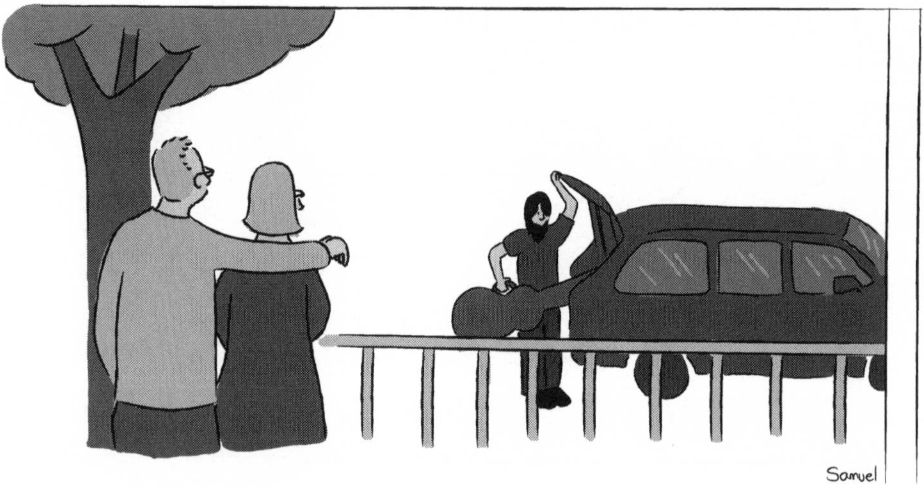
Samuel

"There he goes, endangering our retirement."

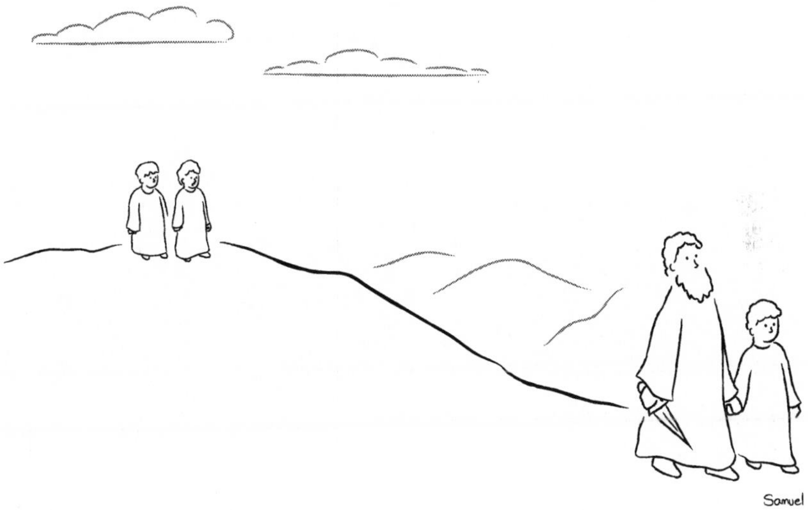
Samuel

"I wish my dad had time off
from work to almost sacrifice me."

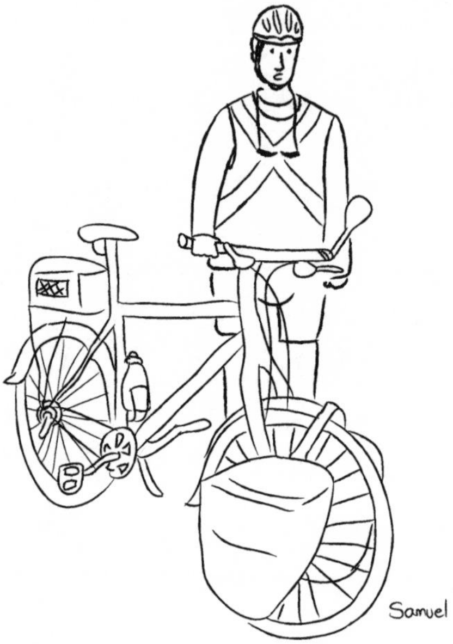
Samuel

"Oh no—I've gone full dad."

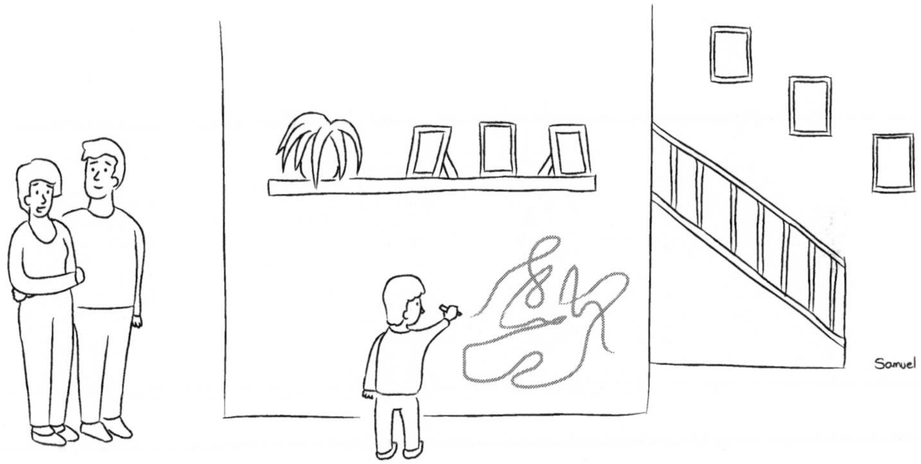
Samuel

"His first street art!"

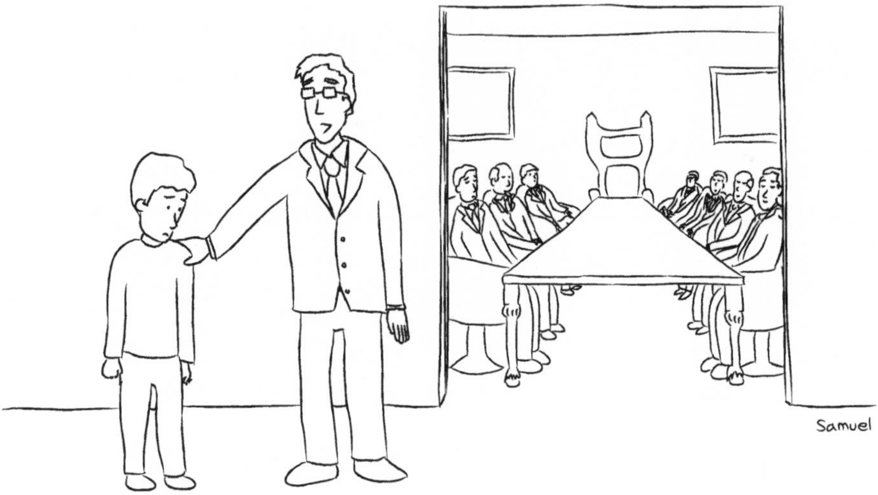
Samuel

"Don't worry son—one day you'll have your own oligarchy."

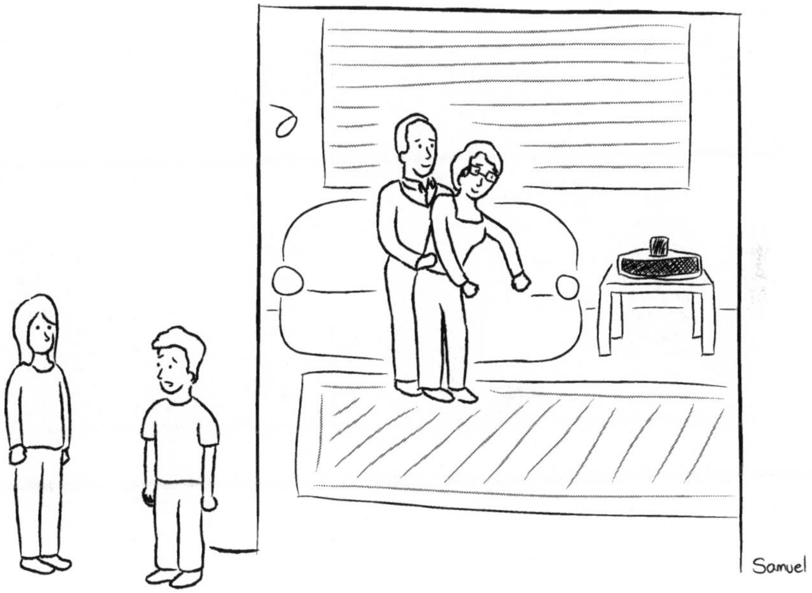
Samuel

"I hate it when Mom and Dad grind."

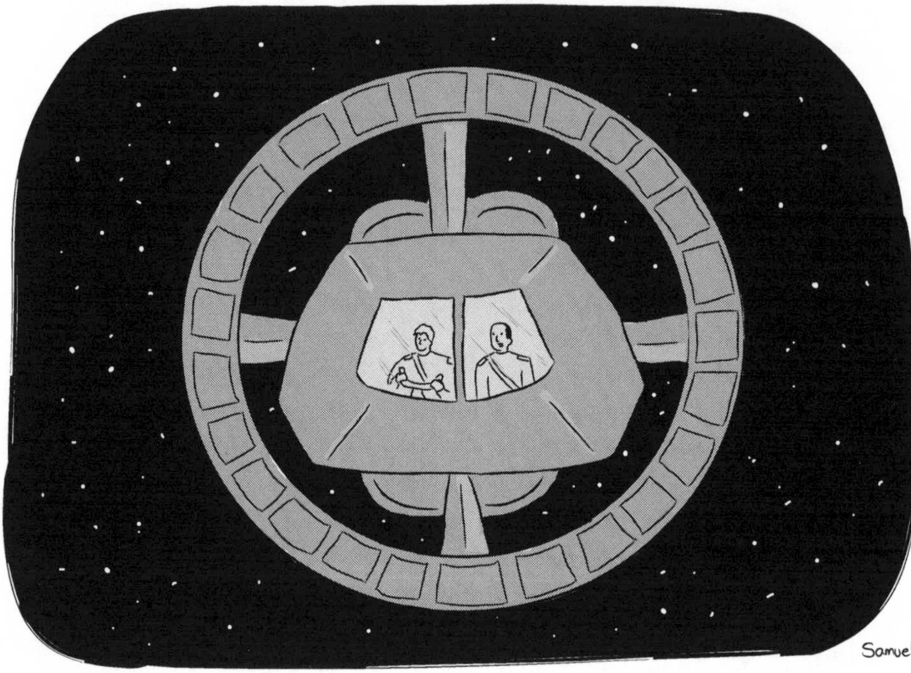
Samuel

"Before you hit warp speed, remember to check your blind spot."

History

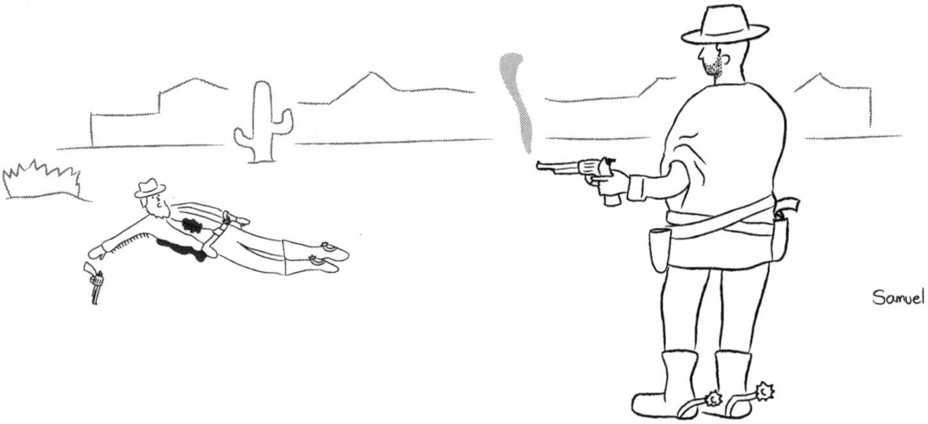
Samuel

"Best two out of three?"

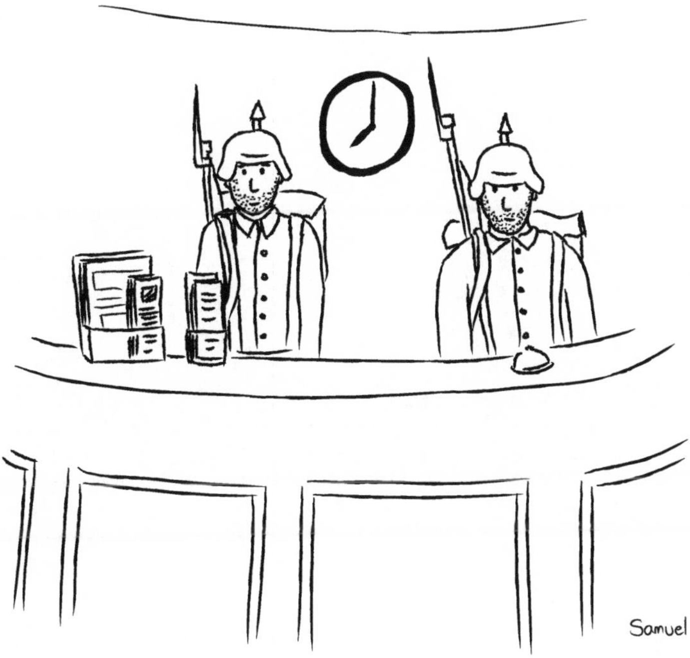
Samuel

All Quiet On The Best Western Front

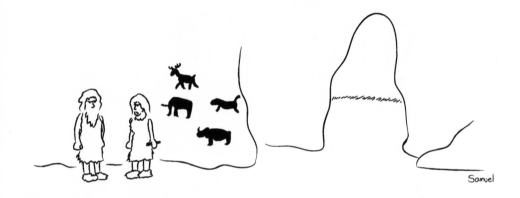

"I thought maybe it would help the environment
if I made a list of endangered species."

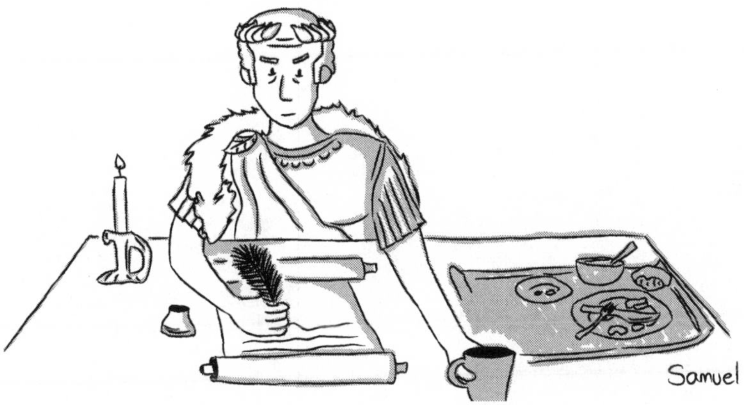
Samuel

I came, I saw, ~~I had a little brunch,~~ I conquered.

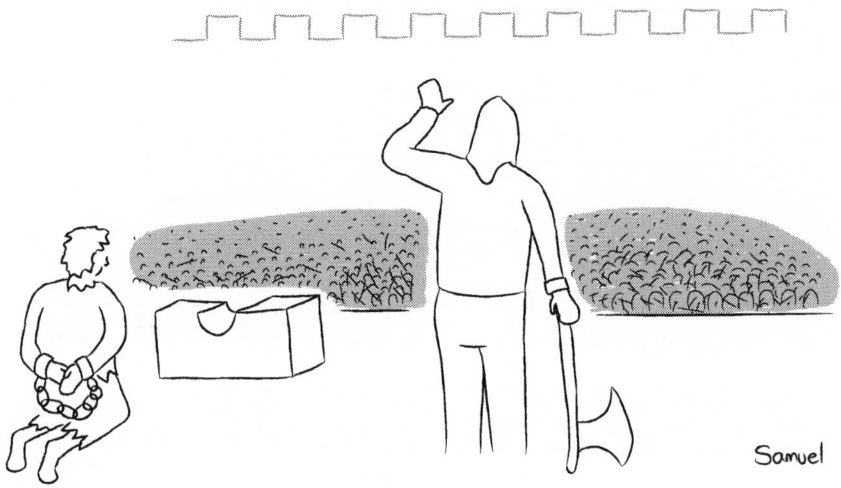
Samuel

"Please hold your applause."

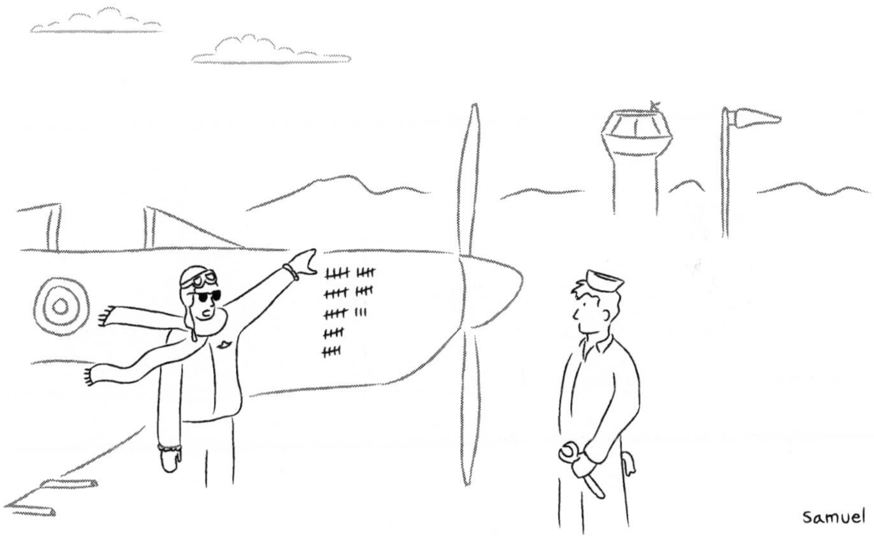
samuel

"Each mark's for a different scarf I've lost."

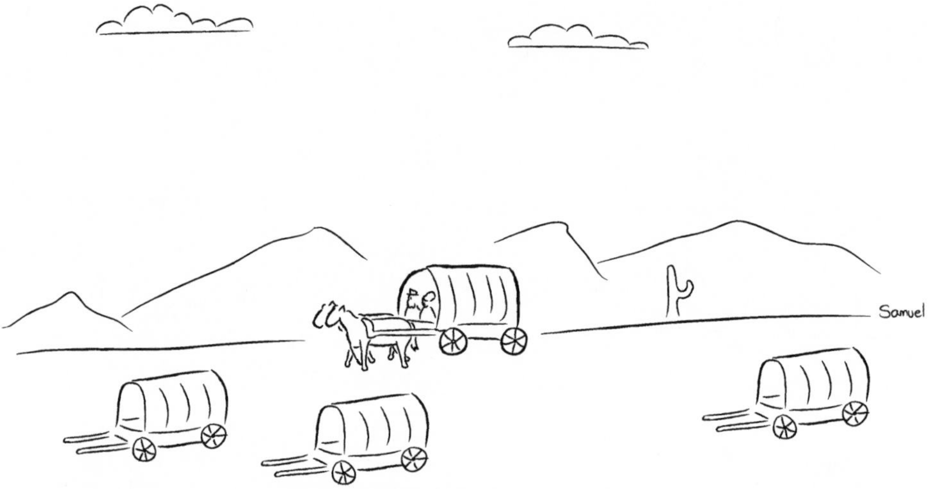
Samuel

"We've already passed two good parking spots."

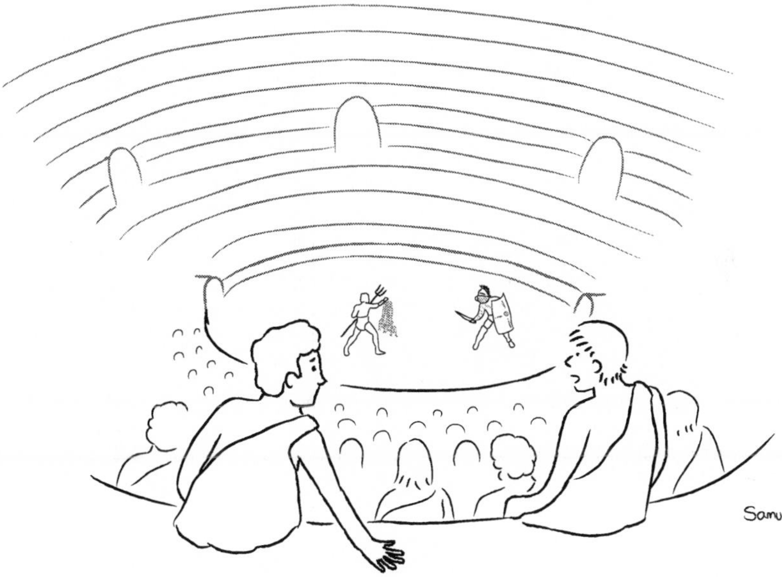
Samuel

"This'll be hard to watch. They're both on my fantasy team."

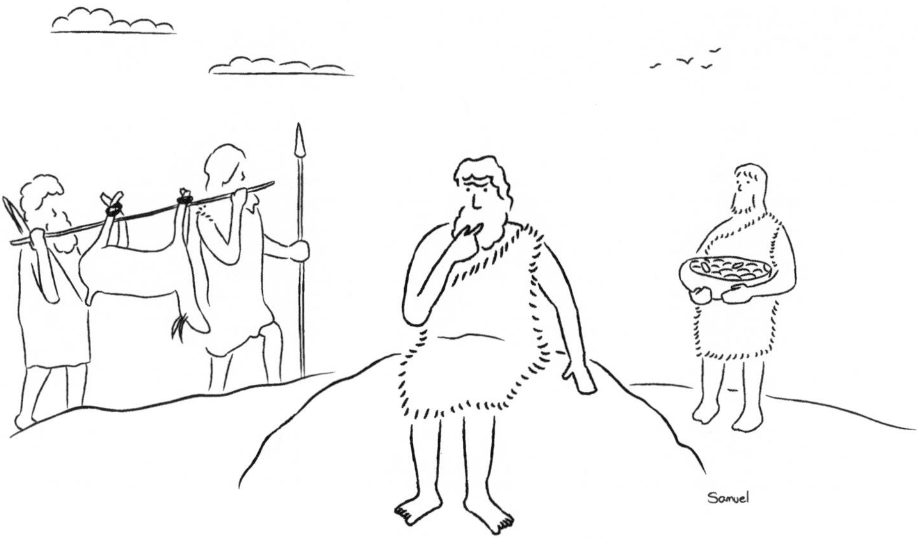
Samuel

Hunter-gatherer-consultant

The Earls of Sandwich

Samuel

81

"Stop trying to reinvent the rock."

Samuel

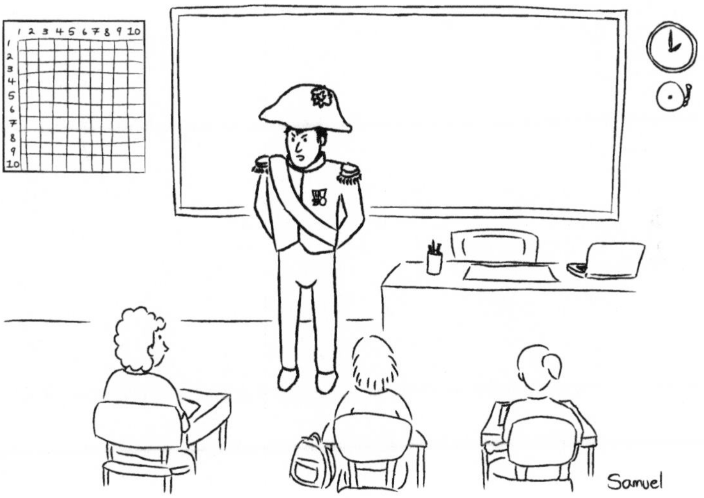
1 2 3 4 5 6 7 8 9 10
Samuel

"This semester we'll learn to add, subtract, multiply, divide, and conquer."

Armchair General

Bathtub Admiral

Samuel

Balloon Cluster Wing Commander

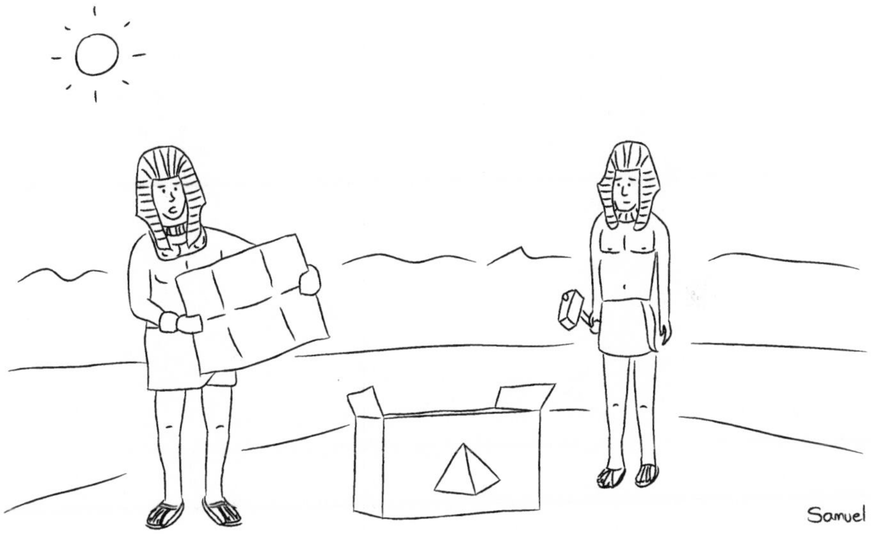
Samuel

"Step one: mass enslavement."

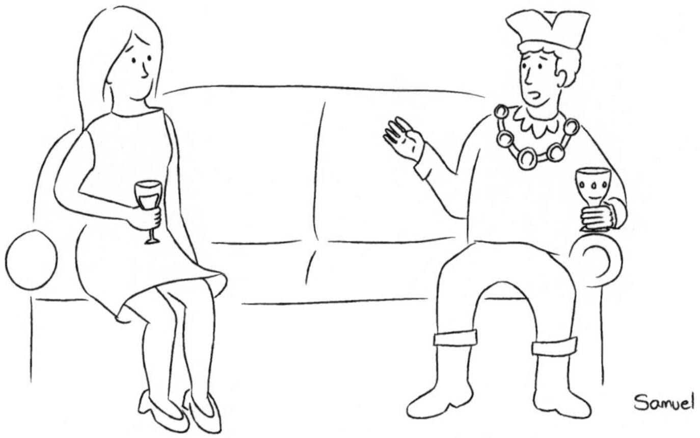
Samuel

"No I'm not a rapper.
I'm just really into mercantilism."

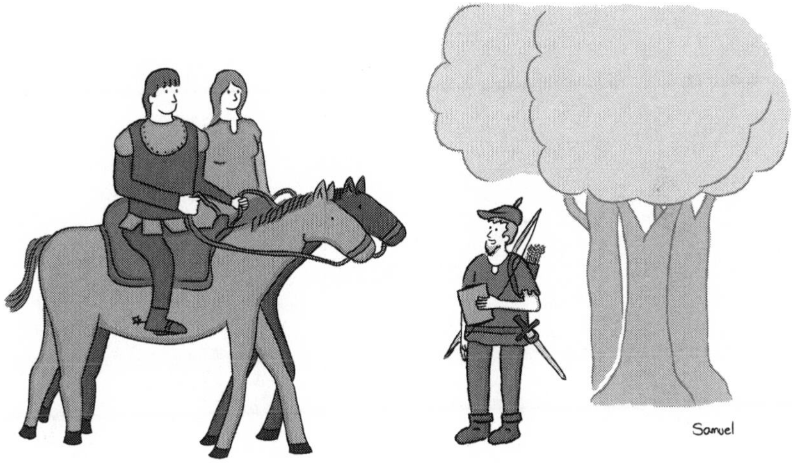
Samuel

"Do you have five minutes to talk about taking from the rich to give to the poor?"

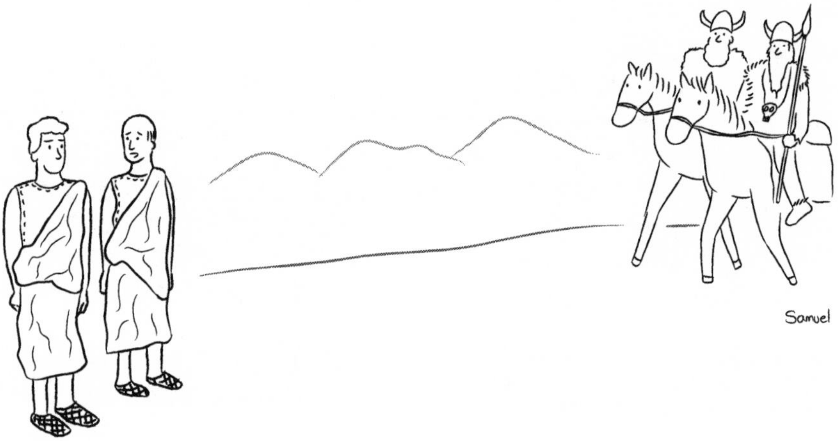
Samuel

"And don't say 'barbarian.' That's their word."

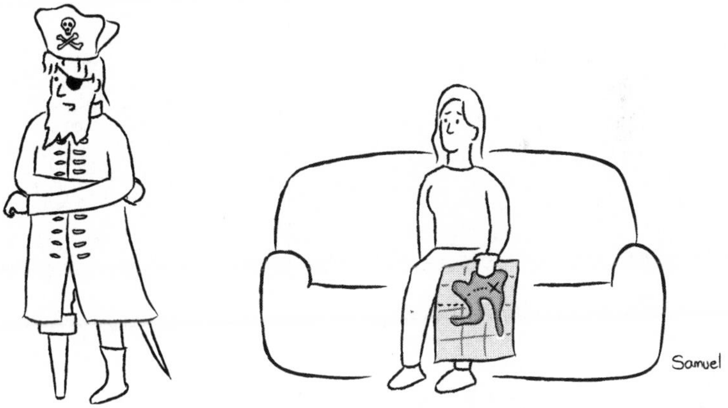
Samuel

"I told you I don't do that kind of thing anymore."

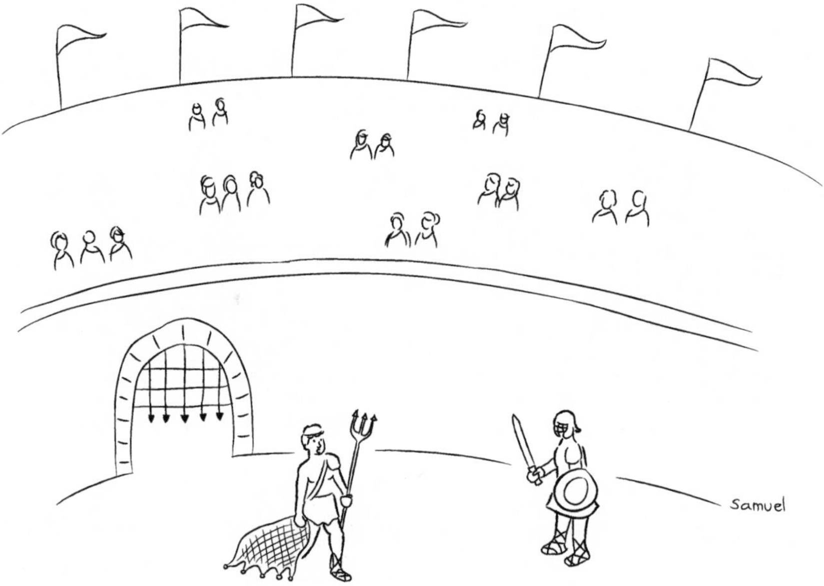
Samuel

"What's our safe word?"

The Internet

Samuel

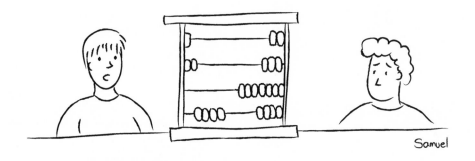

"What apps does it have?"

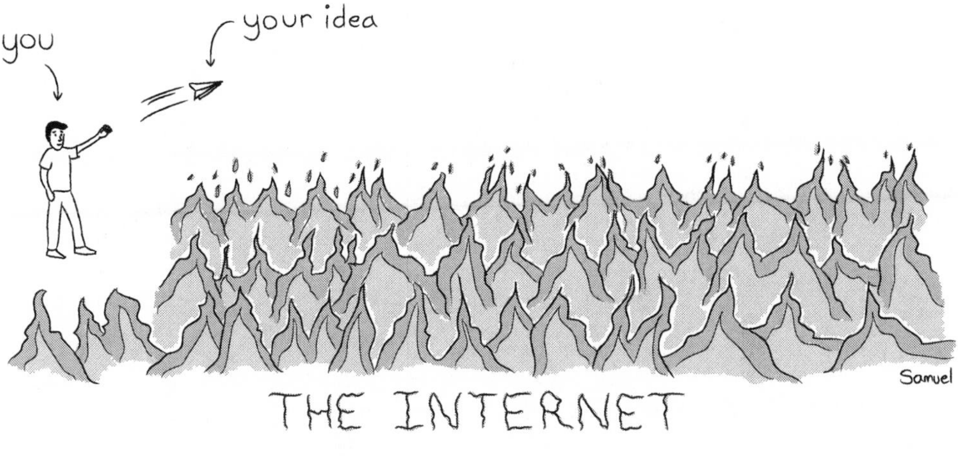
you
your idea
Samuel
THE INTERNET

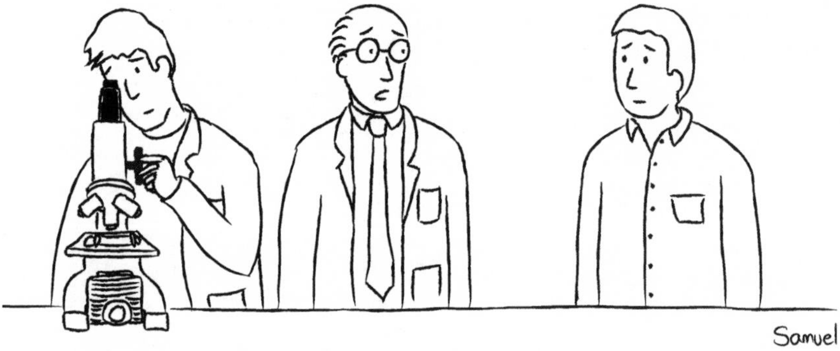
Samuel

"We're almost done analyzing your web presence."

Security Check

Please enter the **two words** below, **separated by a space**, to prove that you are human

Text in the box:

Samuel

Samuel

"I'm tired of always being the hero."

Samuel

"You can't get out of this with a hashtag campaign."

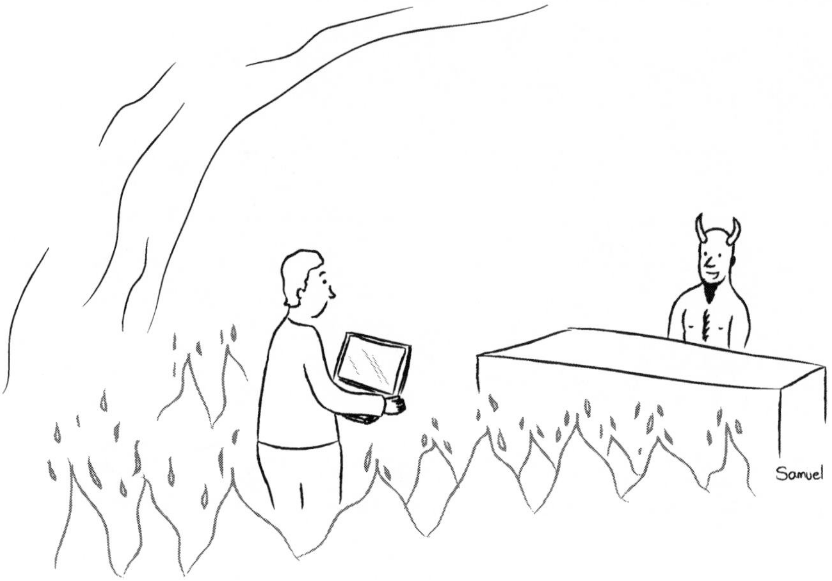
Samuel

"Oh, we don't tell anyone the Wi-Fi password."

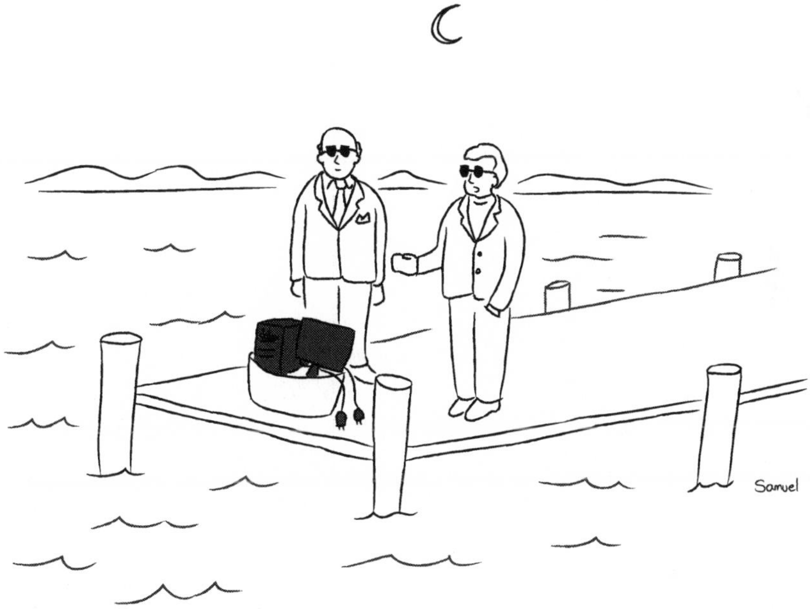
Samuel

"This should take care of my internet history."

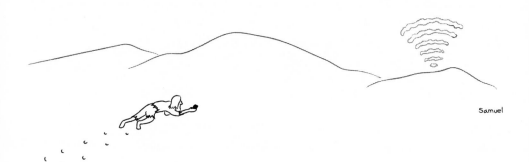

Samuel

100

Personal Growth

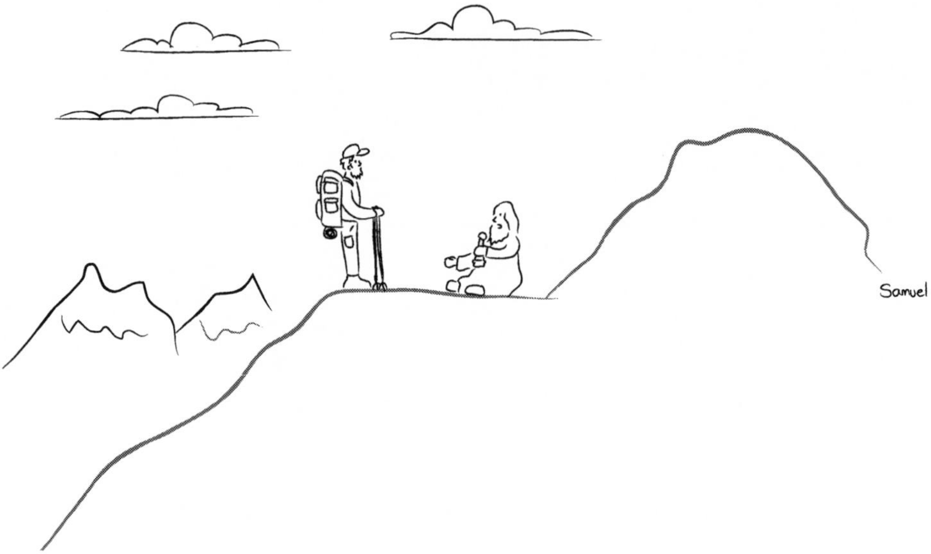
Samuel

"Now that I've told you the meaning of life, would you also like some fresh ground pepper?"

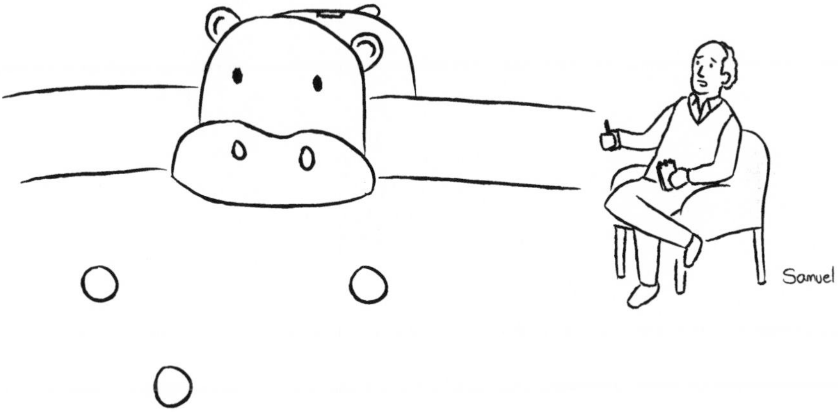
Samuel

"Are you really that hungry,
or are you just eating your emotions?"

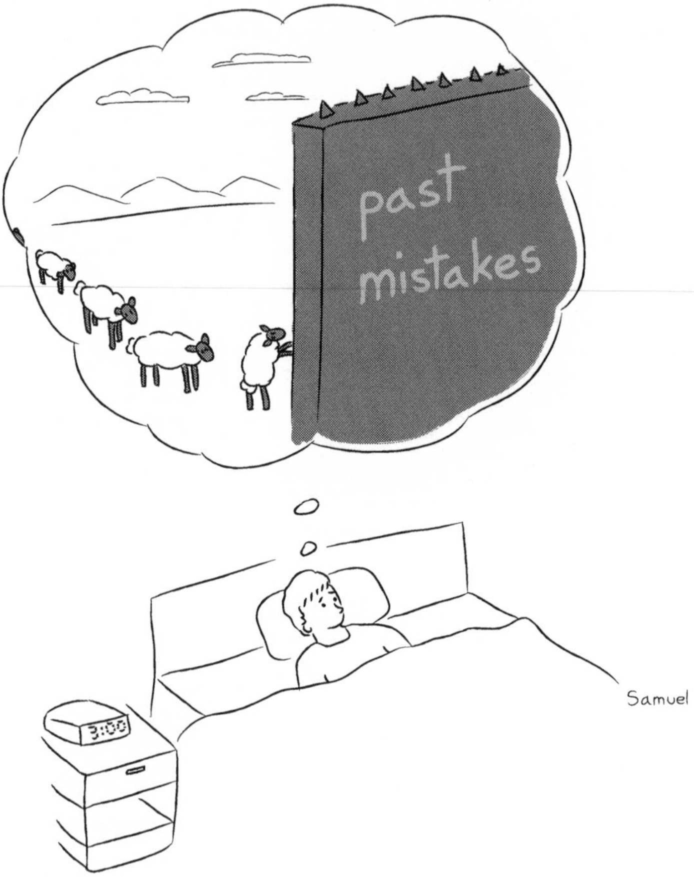
past mistakes
3:00
Samuel

"I'm dressing for the job I want."

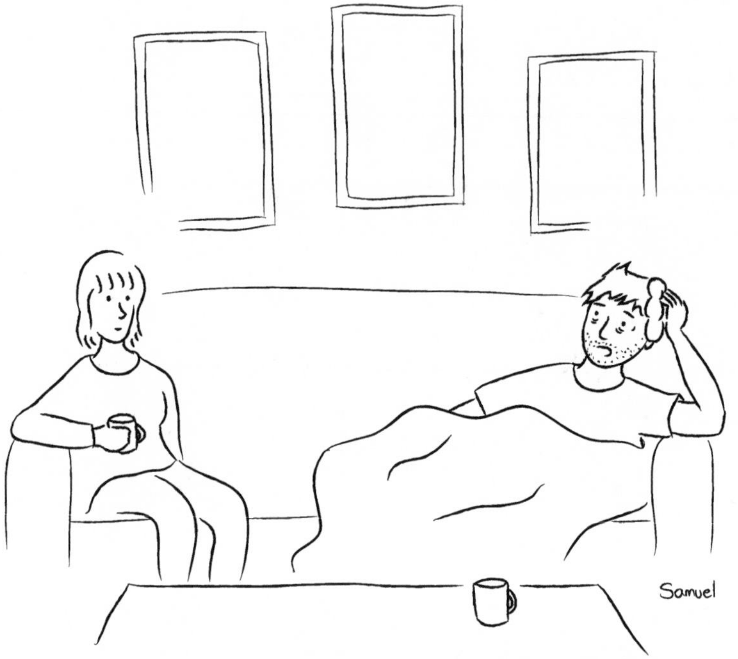
Samuel

"The real hangover is remembering what I said to people."

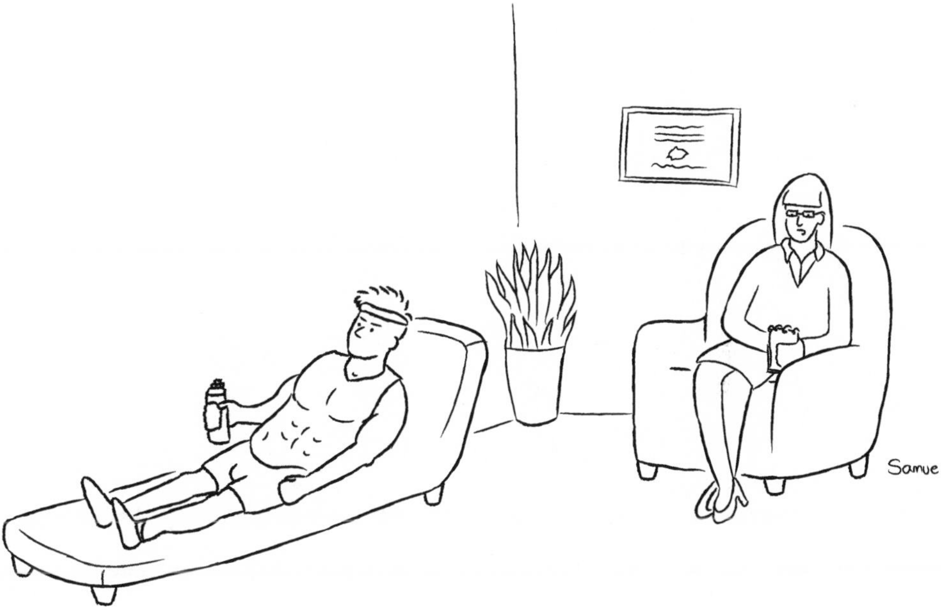
Samue

"You need to start engaging your emotional core."

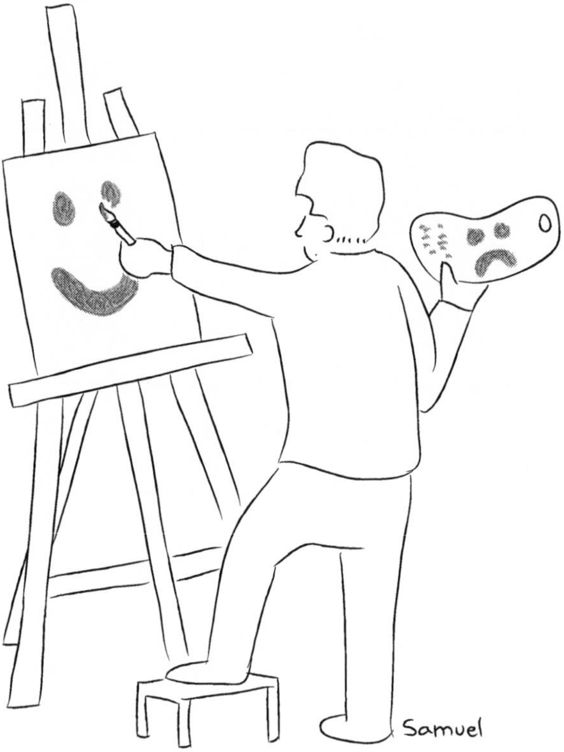
Samuel

And now back to
the adventures of

THE KLUTZ

Samuel

"Foiled yet again by a loose coffee lid."

No longer "simple" machines

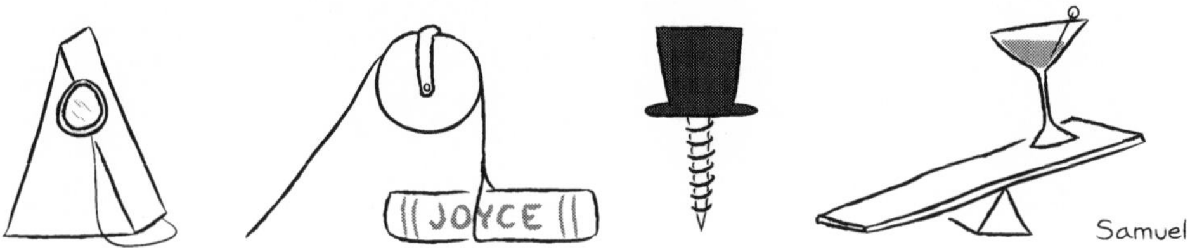
JOYCE
Samuel

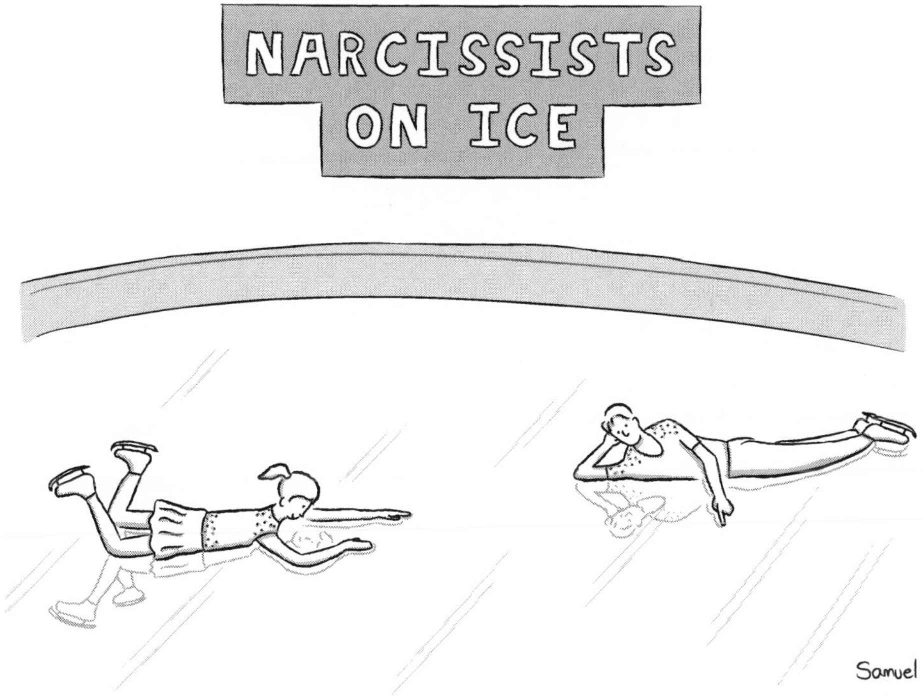
NARCISSISTS ON ICE
Samuel

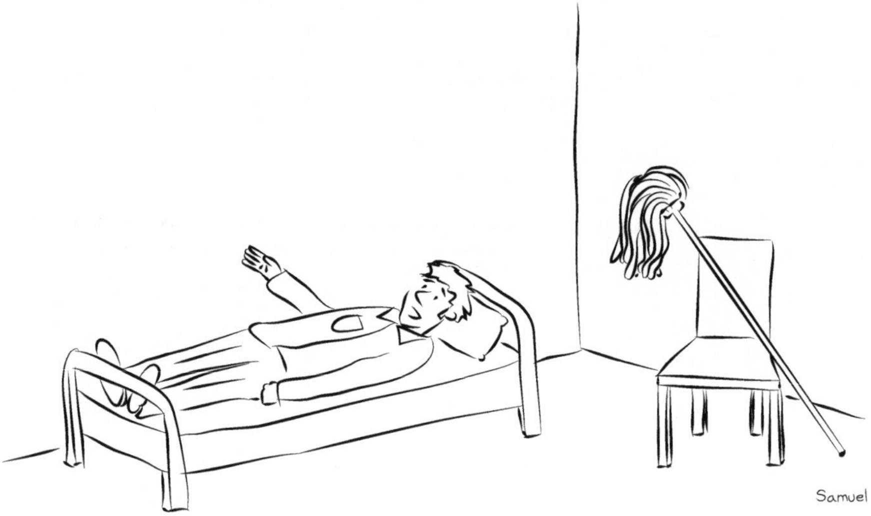
Samuel

"Thankfully, I don't suffer from delusion, doctor."

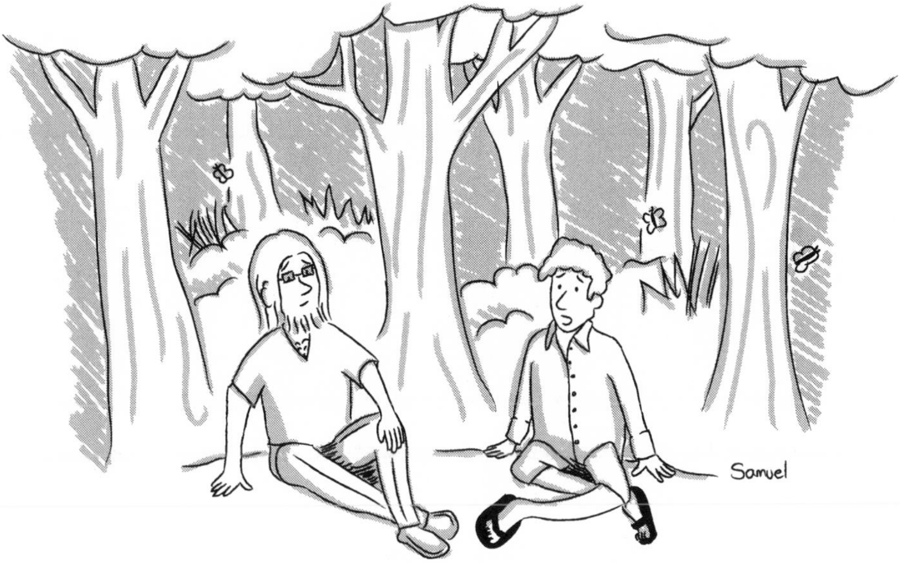
Samuel

"Being out here just isn't the same sober."

SISYPHUS LEARNS TO COPE

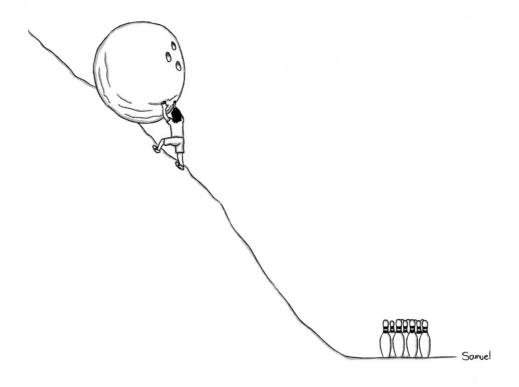

Samuel

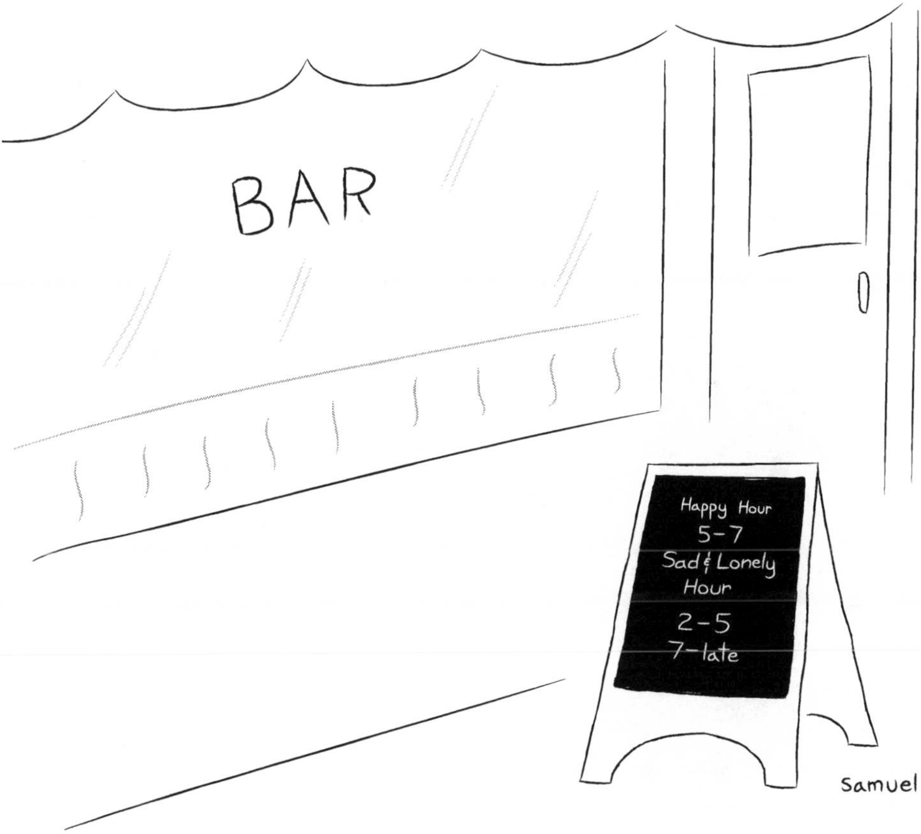
BAR
Happy Hour
5-7
Sad & Lonely
Hour
2-5
7-late
samuel

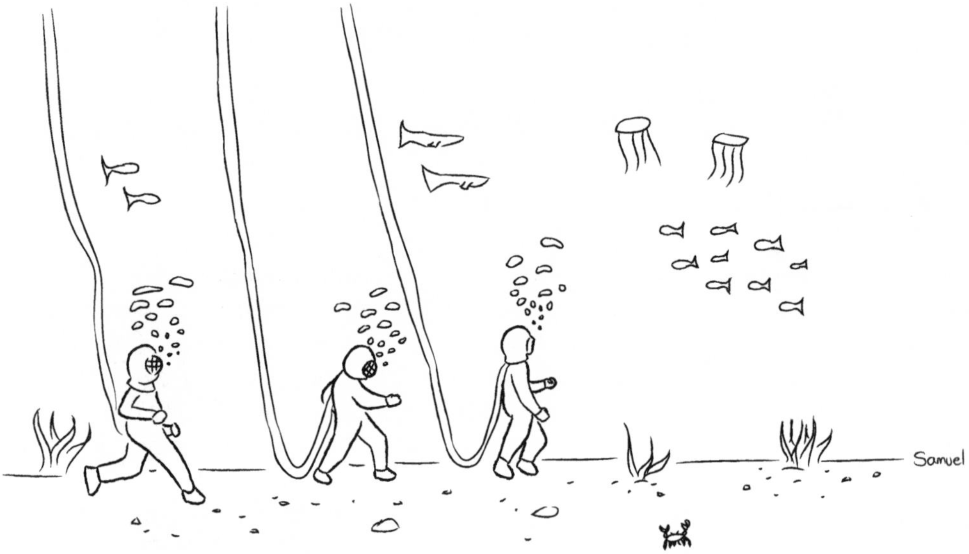
Samuel

Ultra ultra marathon

Samuel

"None of our protein supplements is one hundred percent effective for self-esteem."

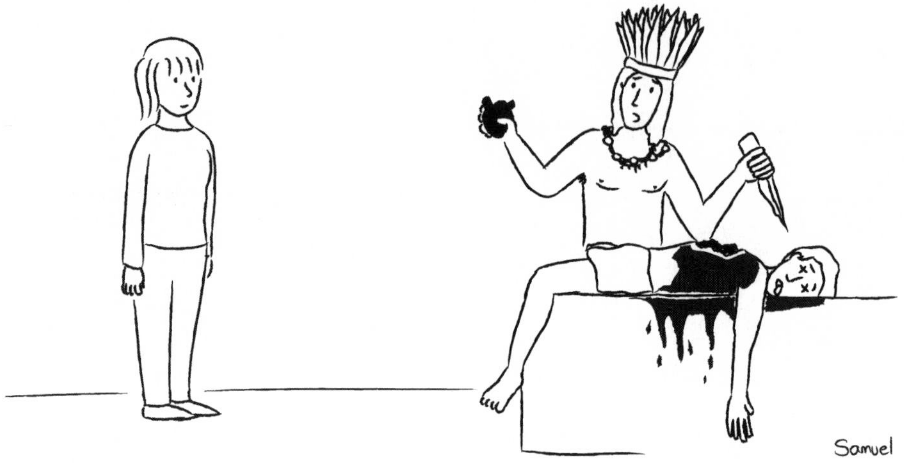
Samuel

"I'm not religious, but I am quite spiritual."

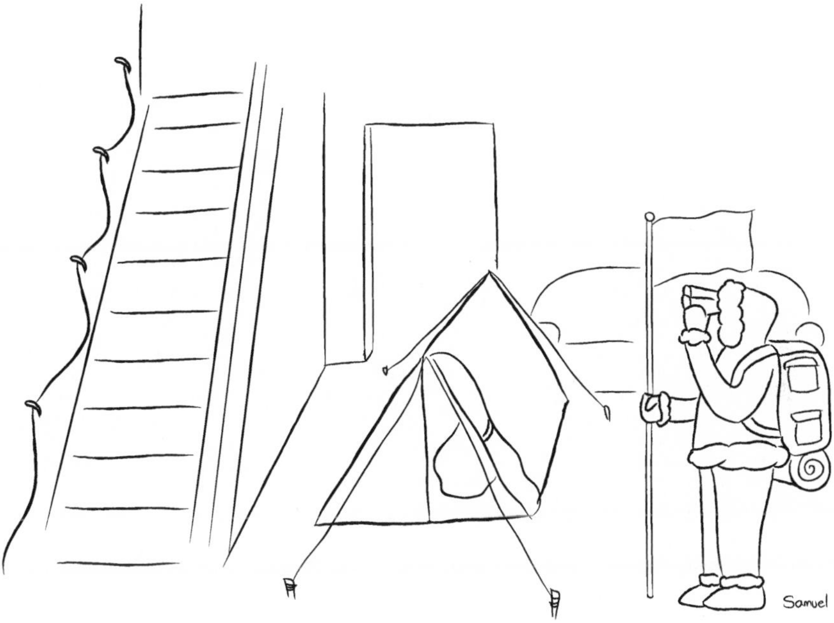
Samuel

Agoraphobic explorer

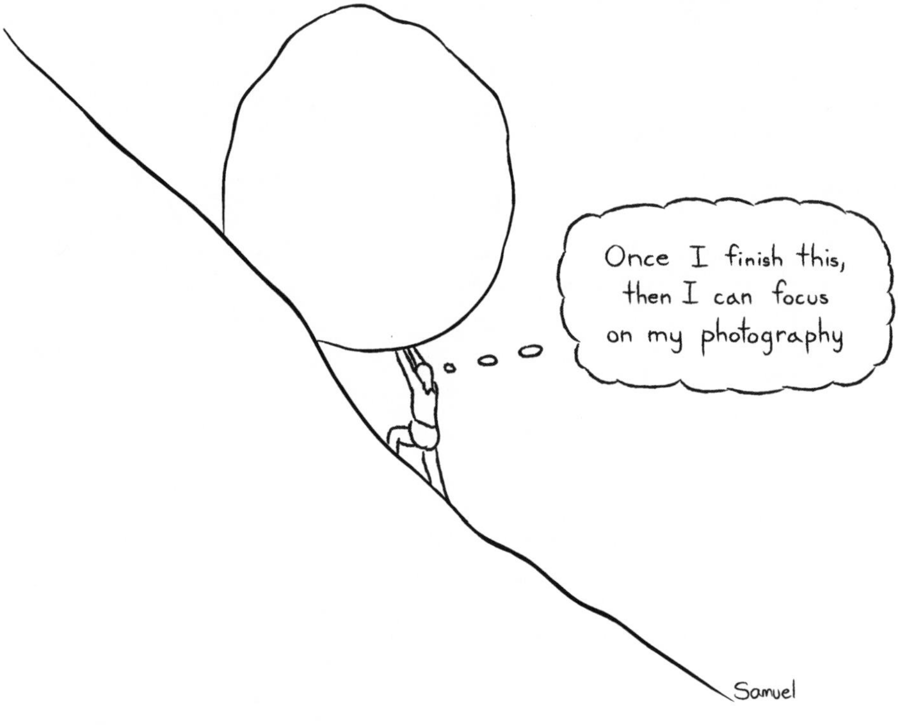
Once I finish this,
then I can focus
on my photography
Samuel

Random

Samuel

More helpful dashboard warning lights

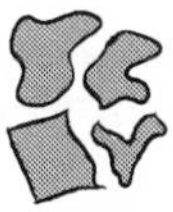

Garbage on the floor has surpassed levels that are socially acceptable

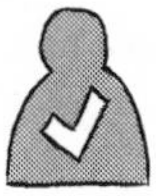

Backseat driver has a point

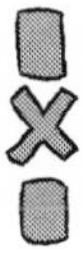

The parallel park you are attempting is impossible

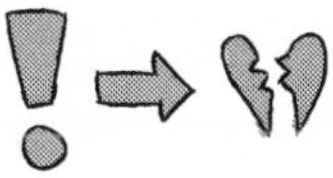

This argument leads to a breakup

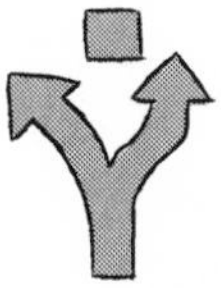

You are about to face a split-second decision about getting drive-thru

Samuel

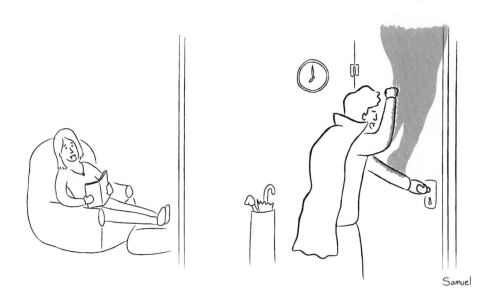

"Why didn't you remind me about daylight savings time?"

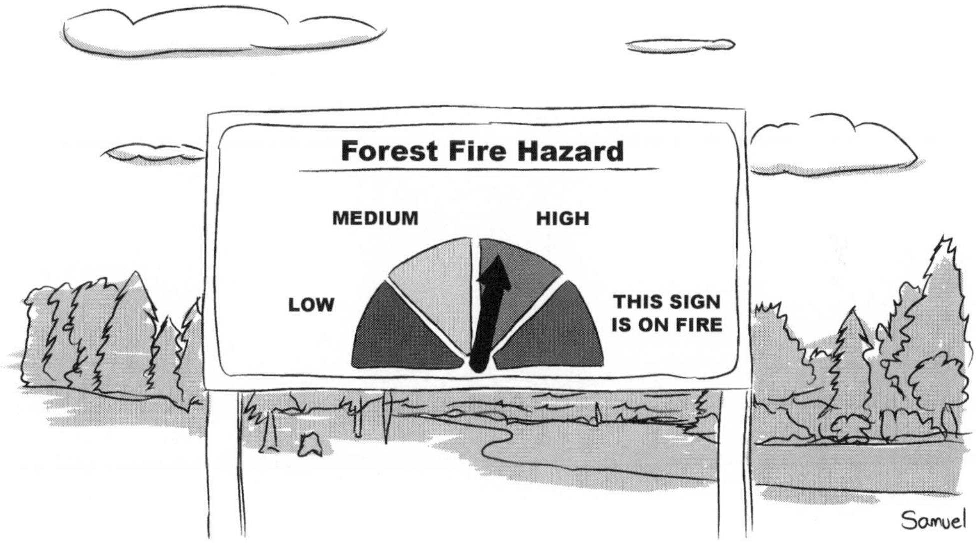
Forest Fire Hazard
LOW
MEDIUM
HIGH
THIS SIGN
IS ON FIRE
Samuel

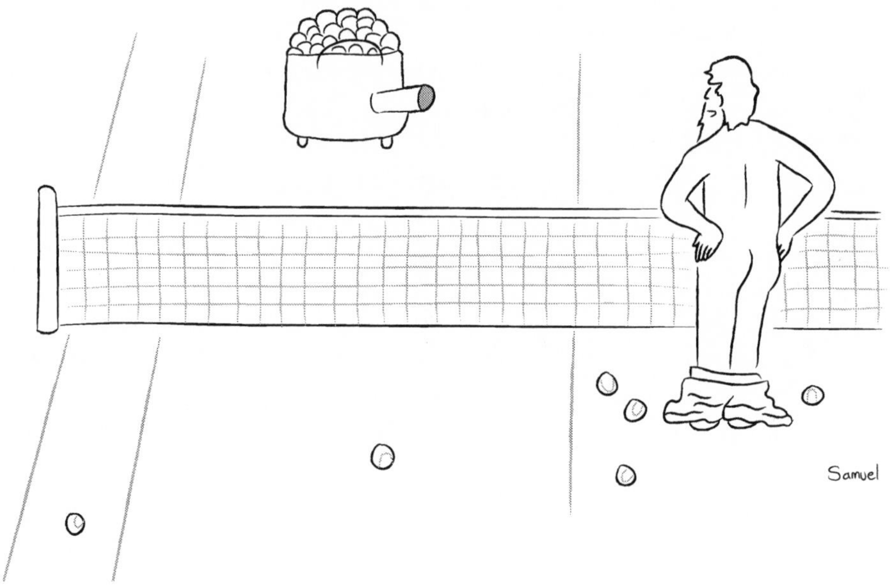
Samuel

"Fifteen–love."

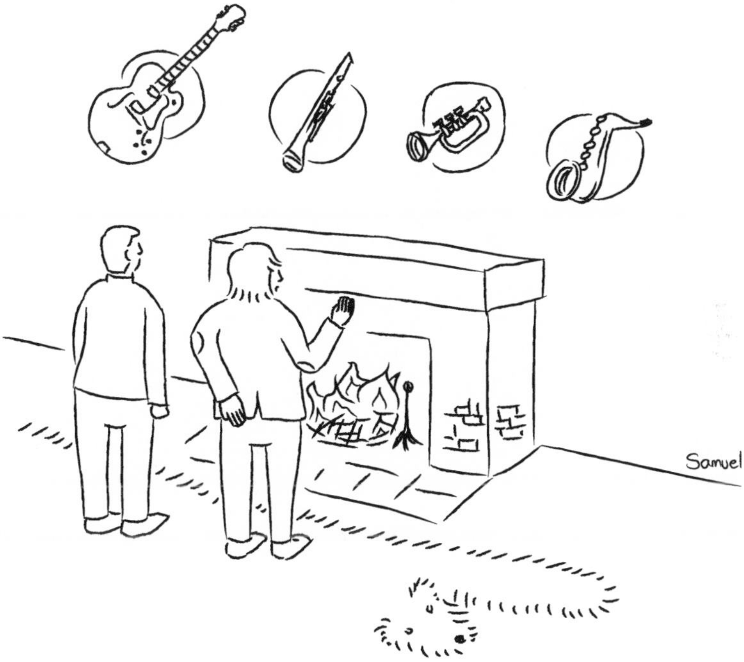
Samuel

"I mainly hunt jazz musicians."

Samuel

Doctor-assisted suicide wings

Relationships

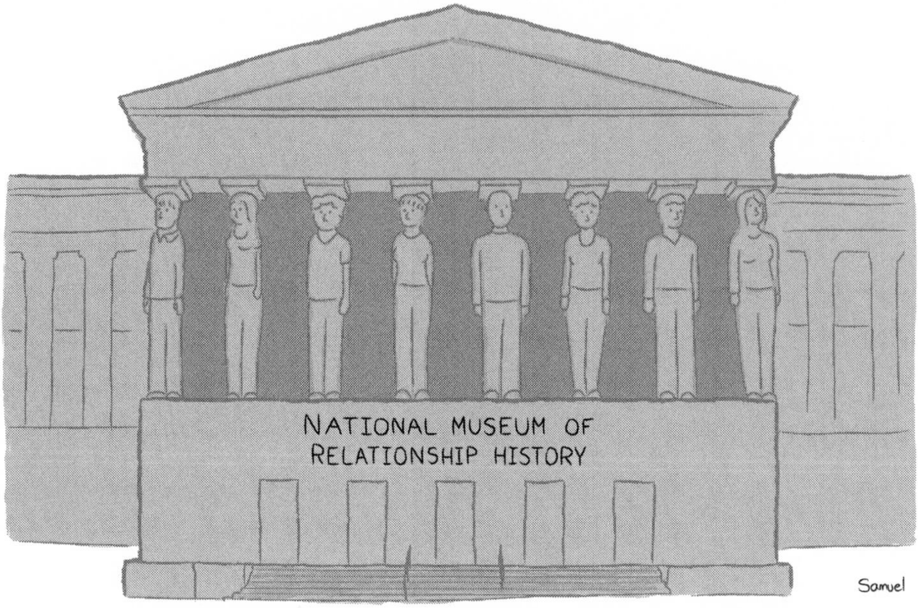
NATIONAL MUSEUM OF
RELATIONSHIP HISTORY
Samuel

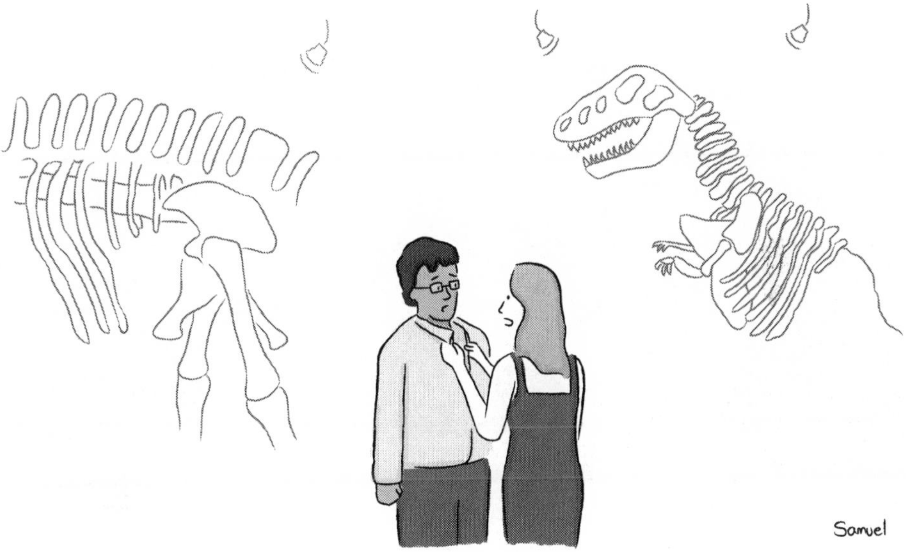
Samuel

"Goddamit Neil! Don't tell me what killed the dinosaurs. Tell me what made them feel alive."

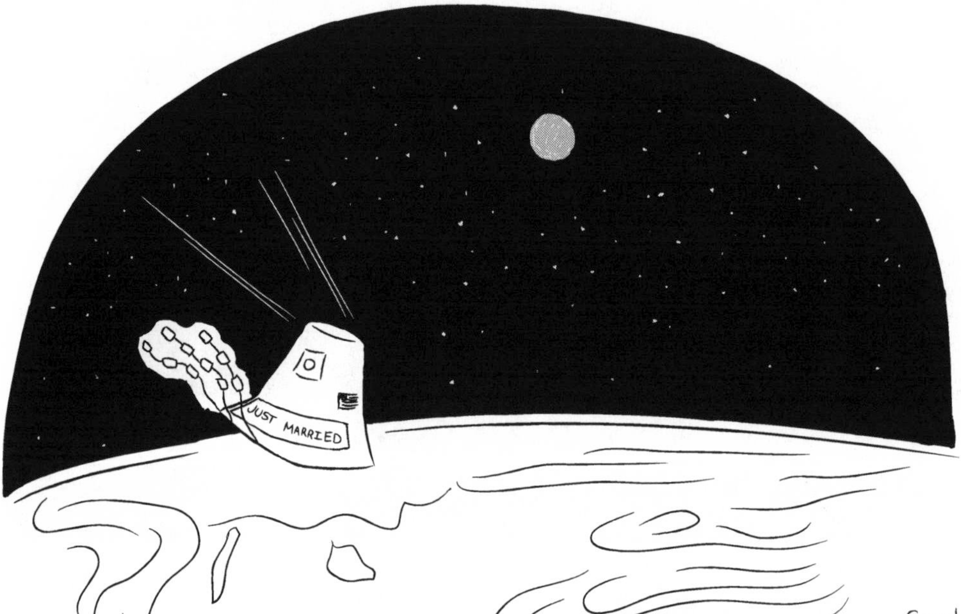
JUST MARRIED
Samuel

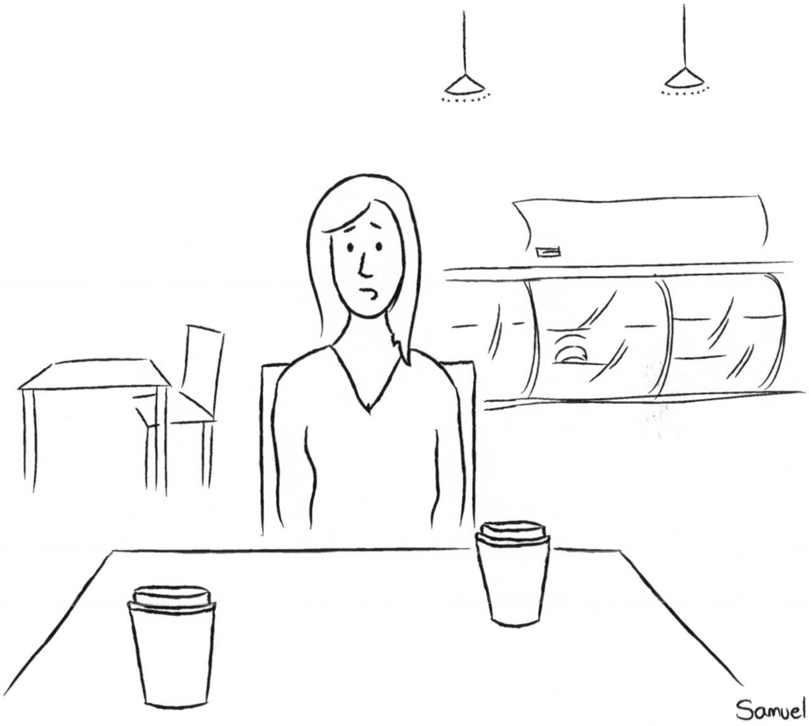
Samuel

"Are you sure you want to GoPro our breakup?"

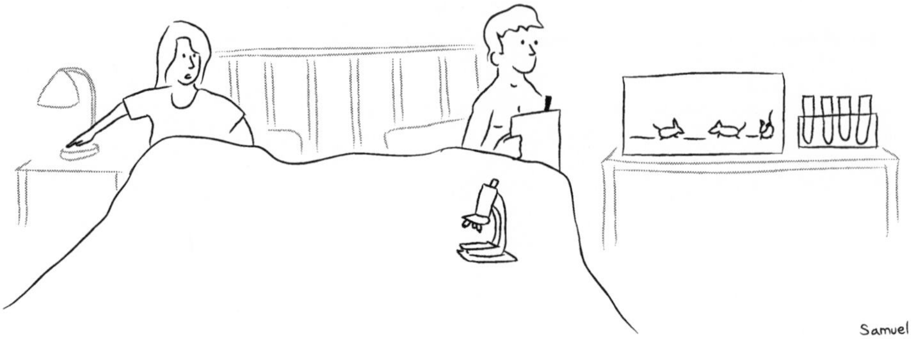
Samuel

"I wish you wouldn't experiment in the bedroom."

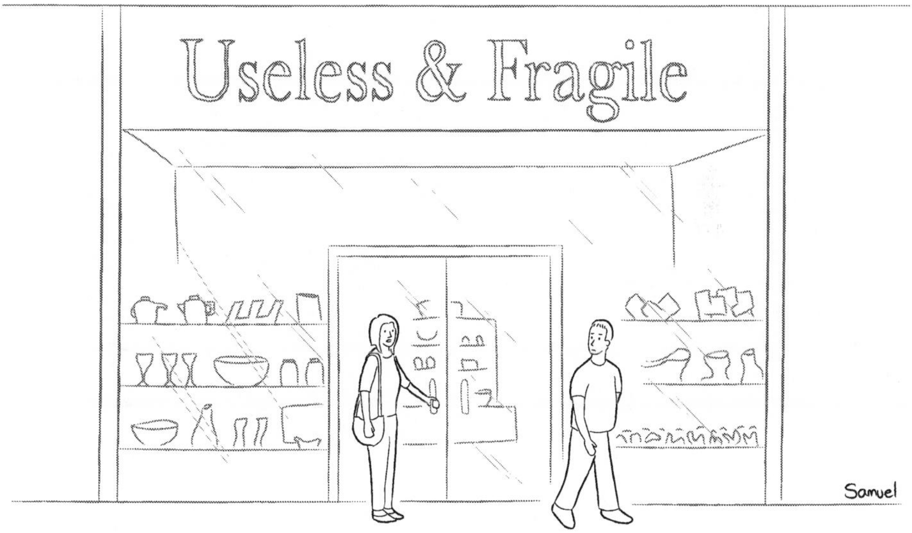
Useless & Fragile
Samuel

"I'll catch up."

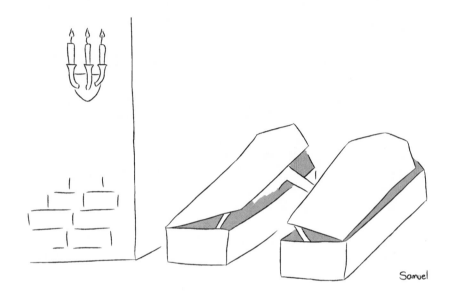

"Not tonight—I have a headache."

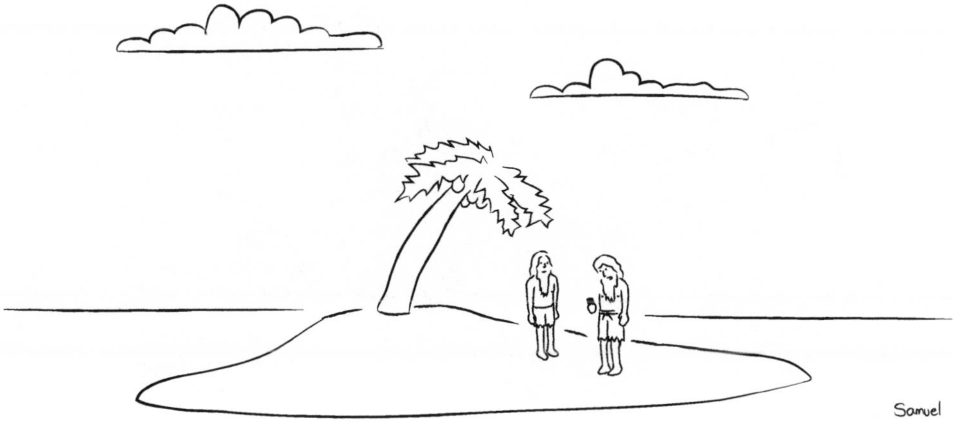
Samuel

"Still no one in our Tinder radius."

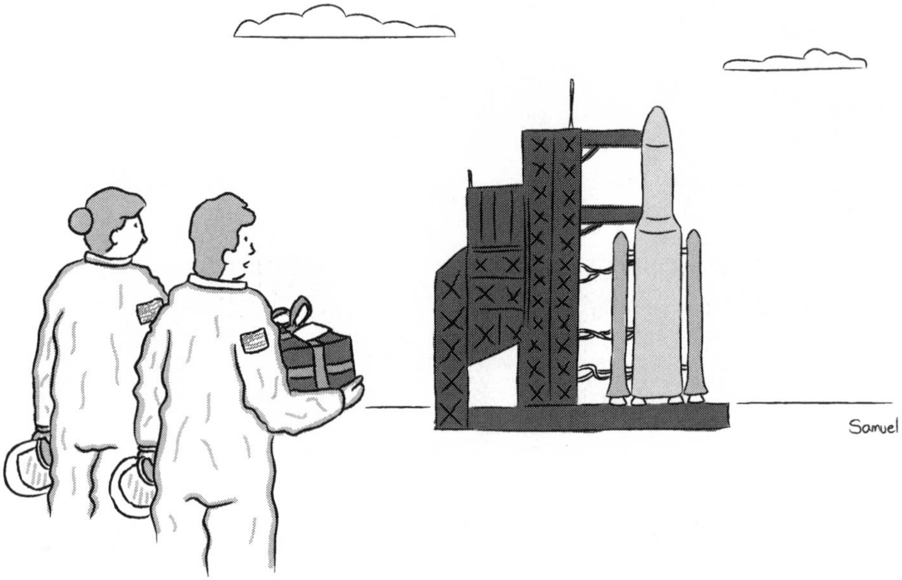
Samuel

"I hate destination weddings."

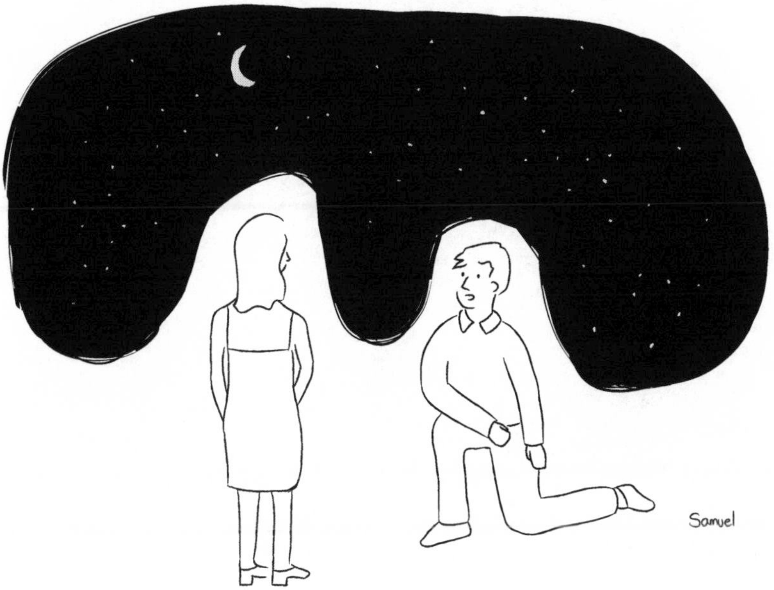
Samuel

"My whole life I've been running from serious relationships, and now I really want to rest my knee."

Samuel

"I thought you loved me for who I am."

Samuel

"All my plays are about how much I want to hug and kiss you."

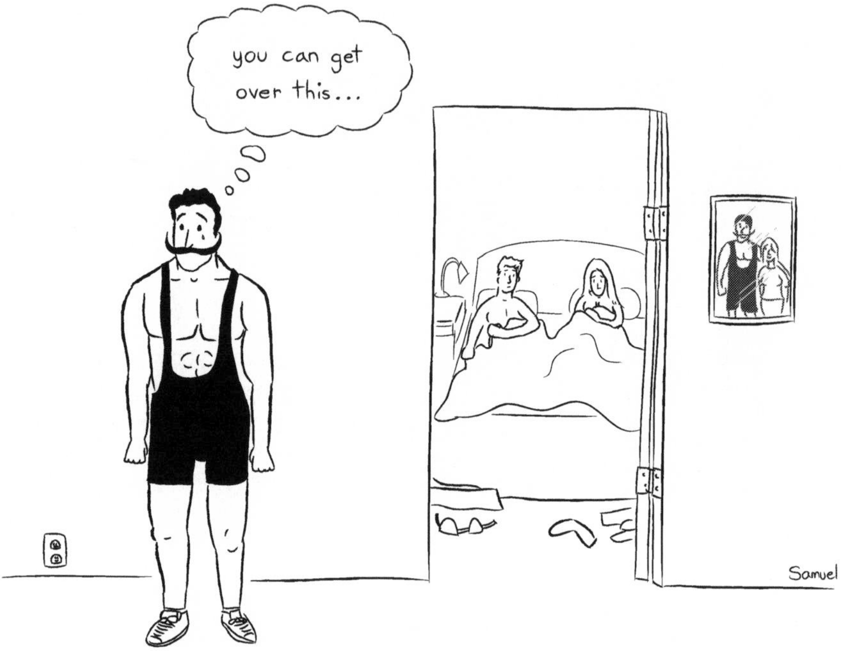
you can get over this...
Samuel

Emotional strongman

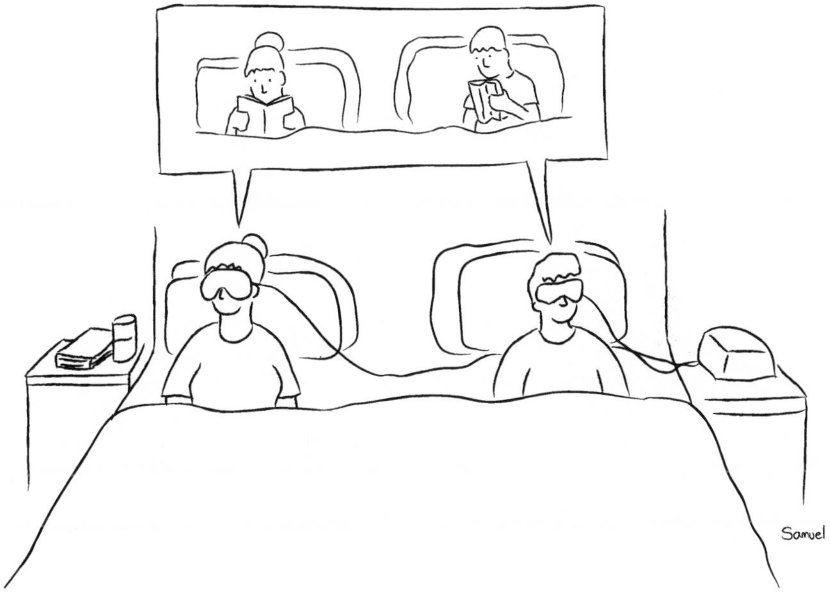
Samuel

Virtual marriage reality

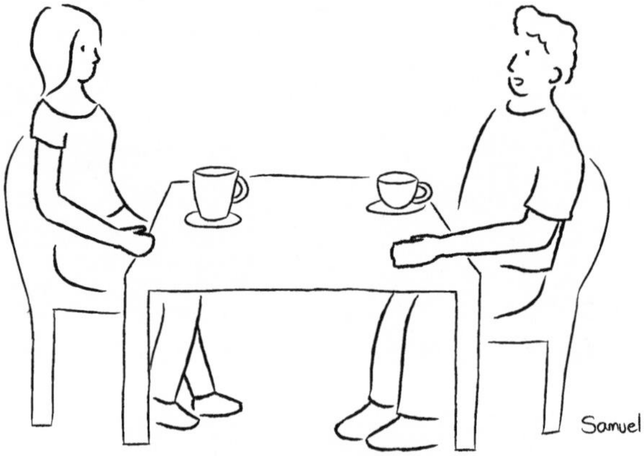
Samuel

"Please be honest with me
in a way that shields me from the truth."

JOHNSON
RACHEL
1991-2075
WIFE
CARL
1988-2068
HUSBAND
85% Compatible
Samuel

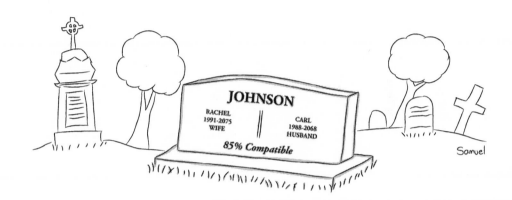

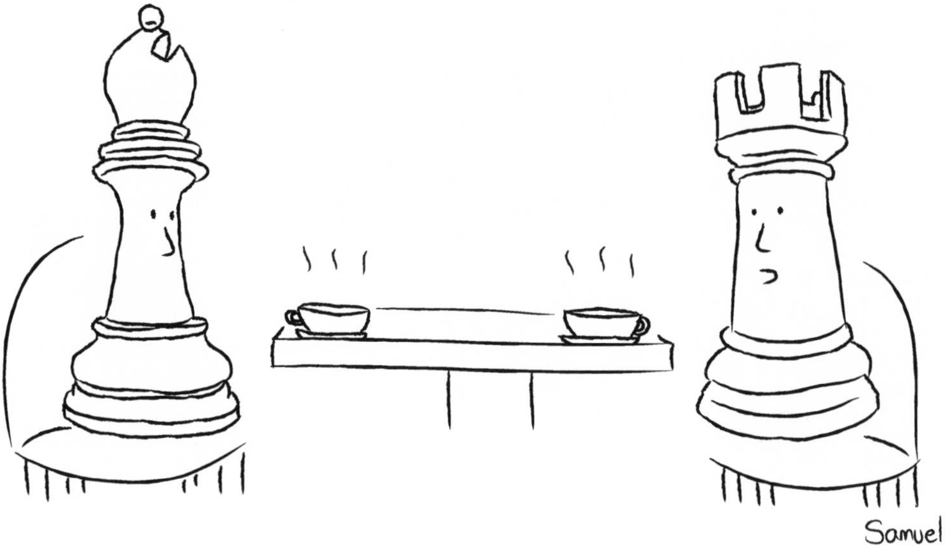
Samuel

"So, you still moving diagonally?"

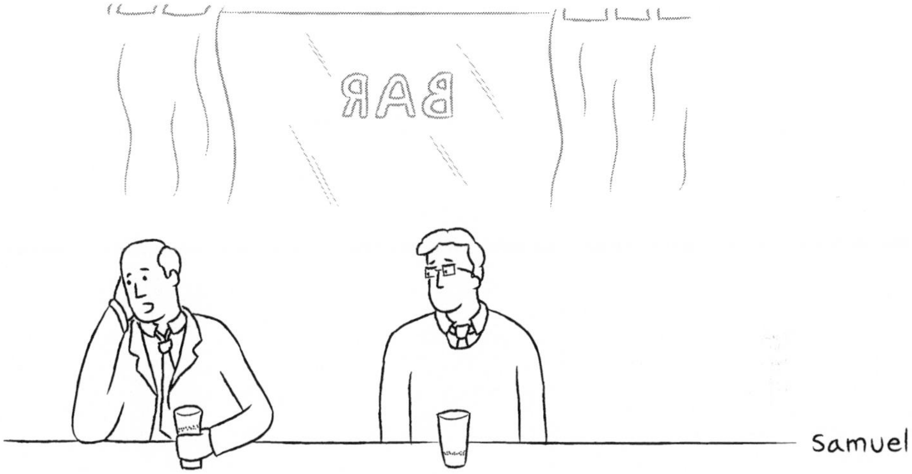
samuel

"I'm suffering through a sexless divorce."

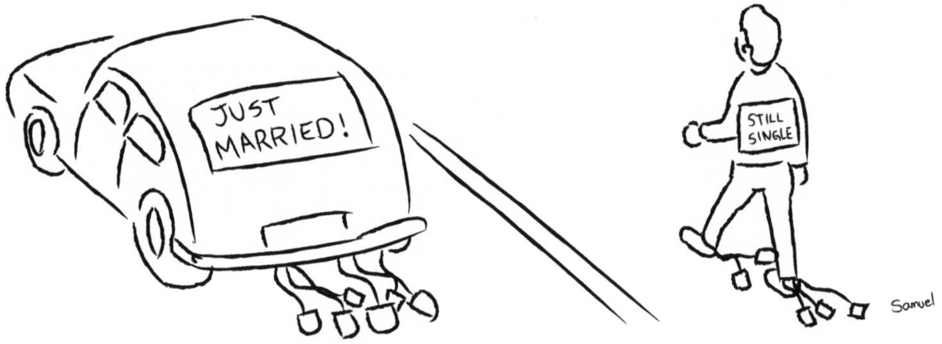
JUST MARRIED!
STILL SINGLE
Samuel

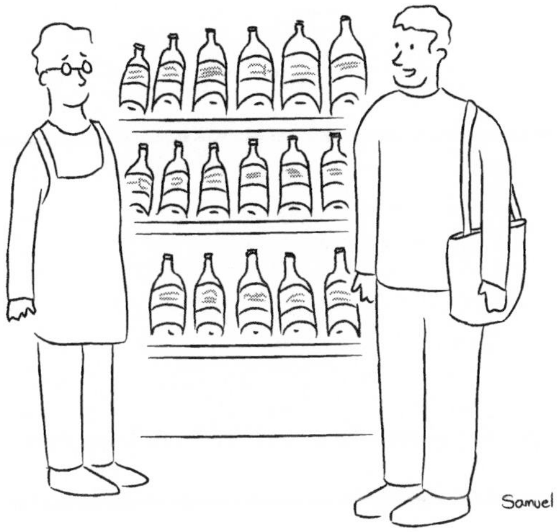
Samuel

"Which wine would you recommend for a failing marriage?"

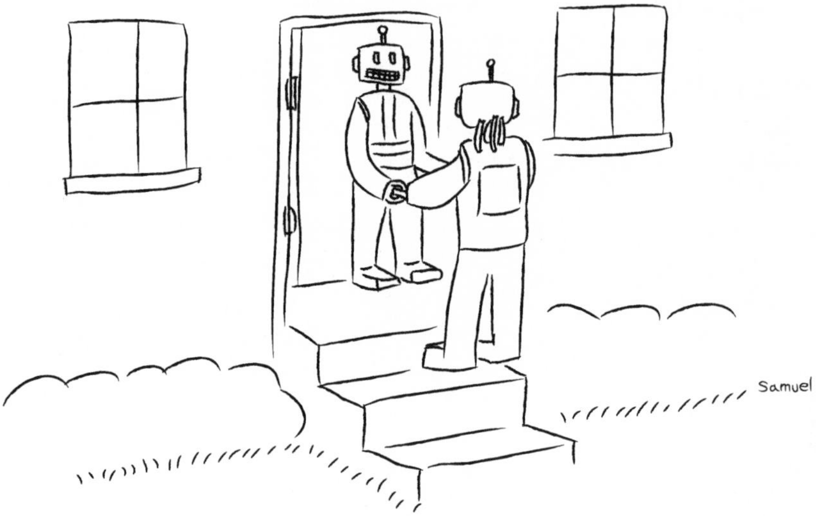
Samuel

"Stop, you had me at 0100100001000101010011000100110001001111."

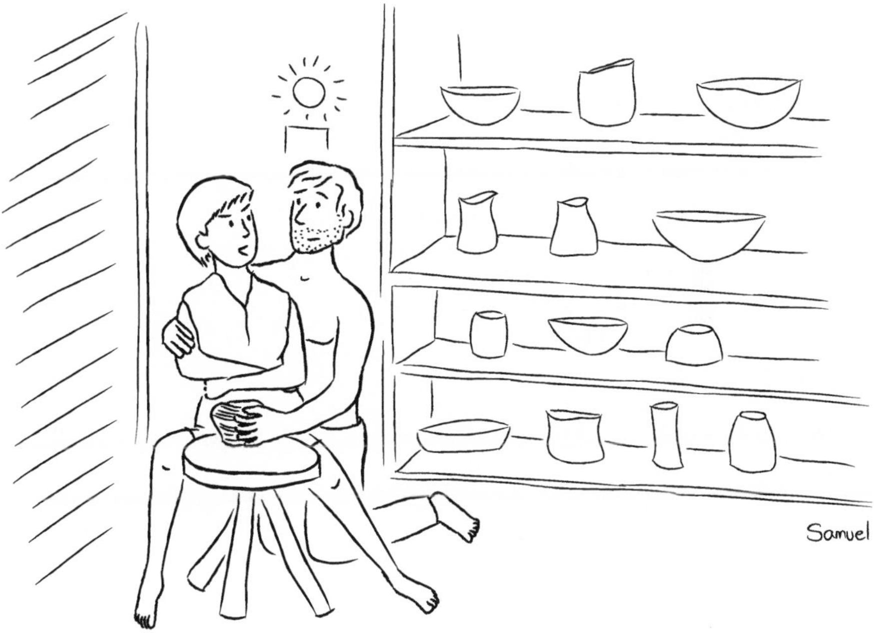
Samuel

"It's not sexy if you ruin my bowl."

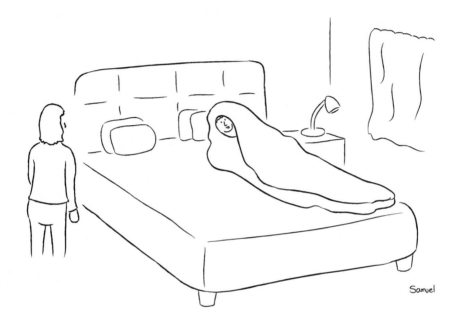

"What's up? I'm in a nap burrito."

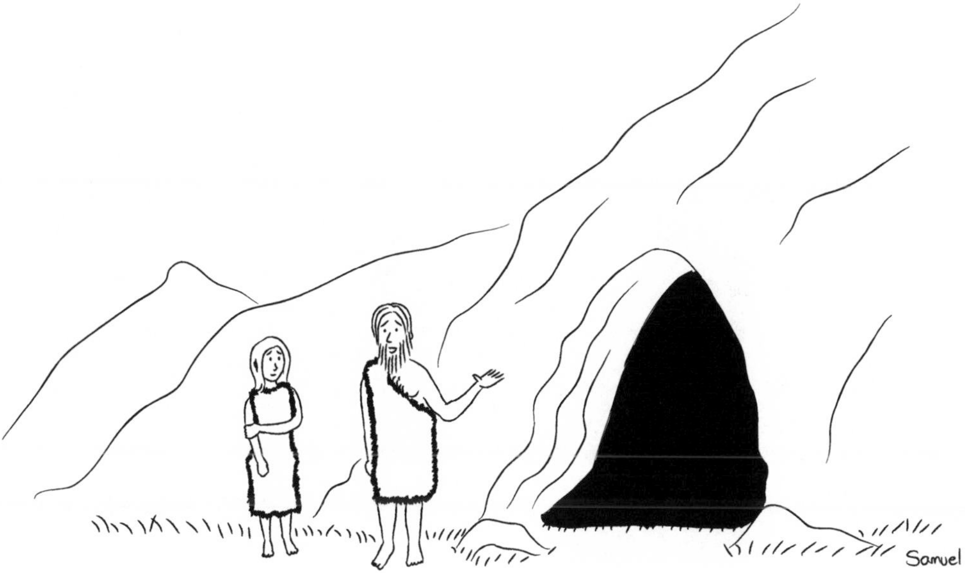
Samuel

"Do you want to come in and watch some fire?"

Samuel

"This is why I wanted to hire movers."

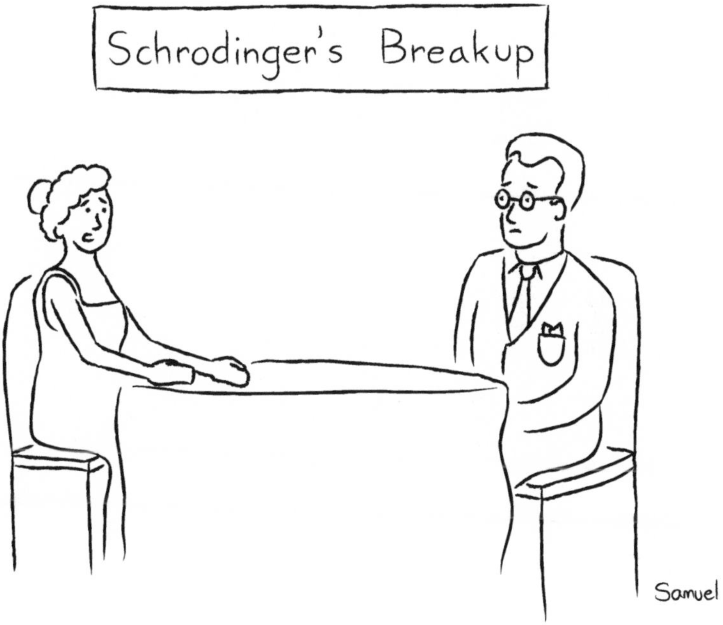
Schrodinger's Breakup
Samuel

"It's you and it's me."

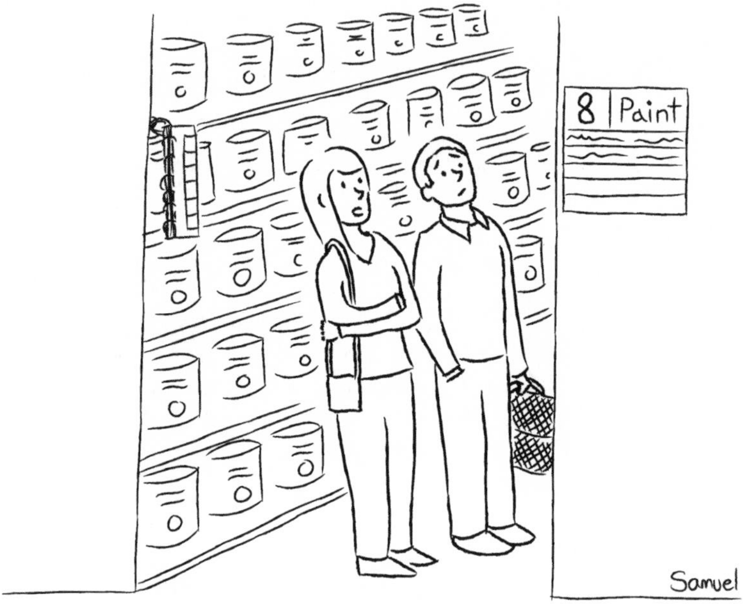
8 Paint
Samuel

"At least make a suggestion so I have something to say no to."

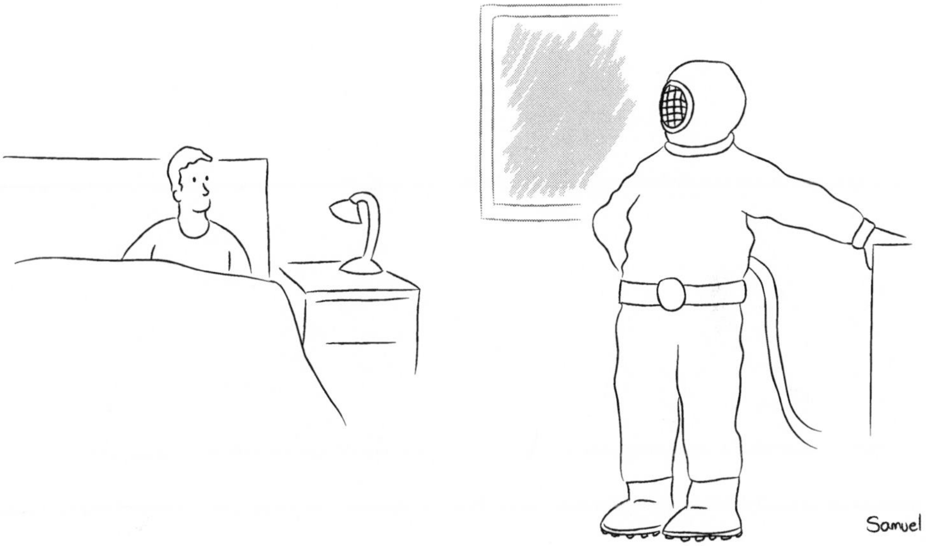
Samuel

"Let me slip into something more comfortable."

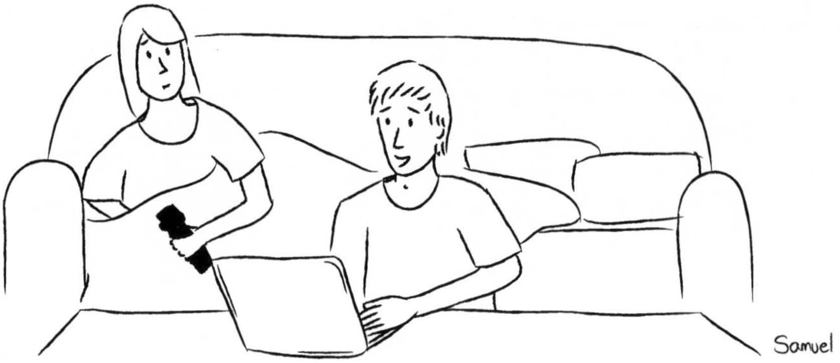
Samuel

"The wedding photographer really captured your temper tantrum."

Science

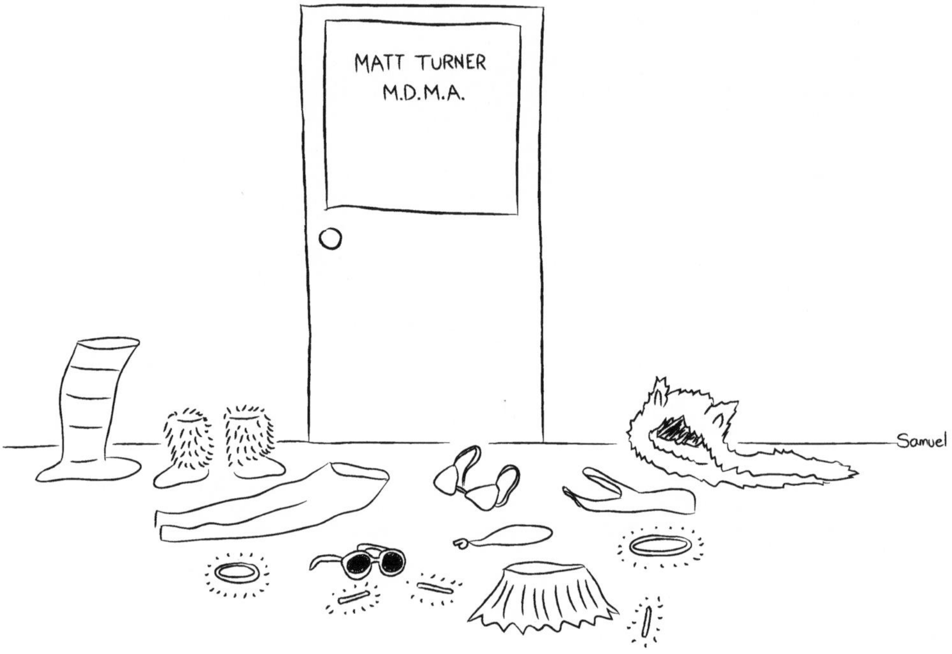
MATT TURNER
M.D.M.A.
Samuel

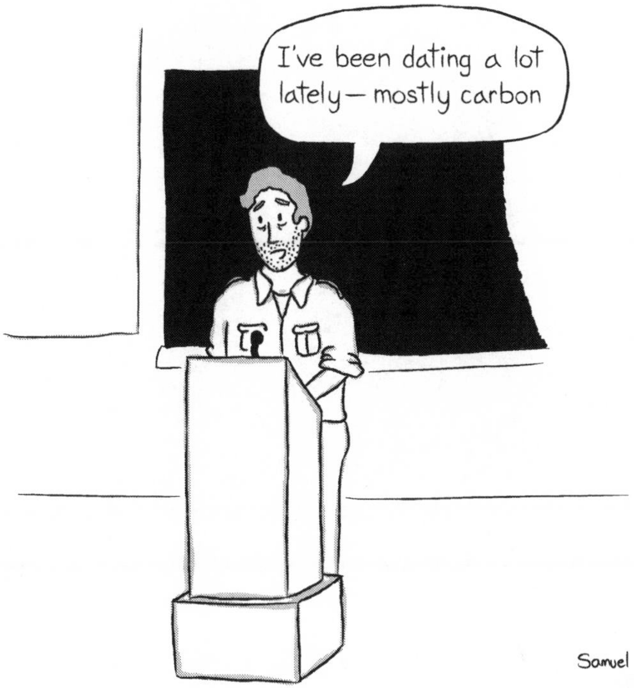
I've been dating a lot lately— mostly carbon
Samuel

The Loneliest Archaeologist

Samuel

Multinational Space Station

162

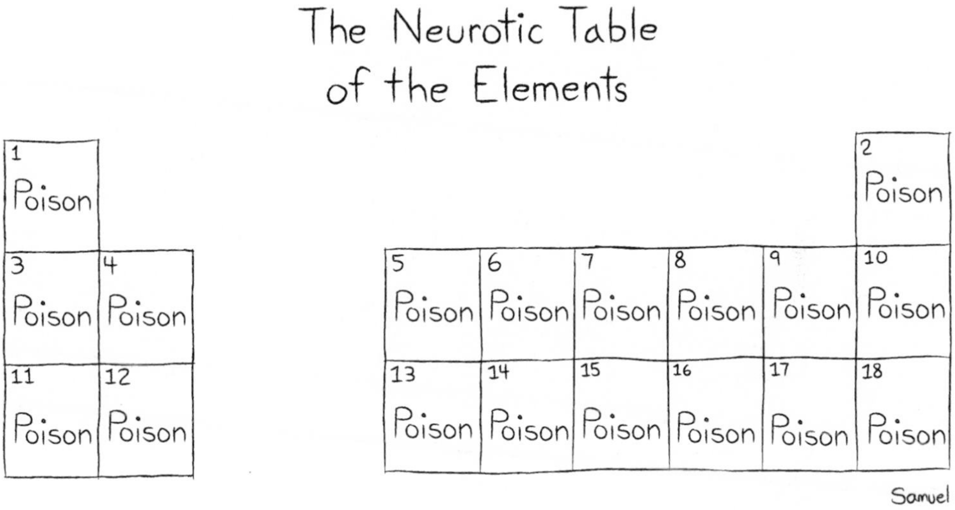

The Neurotic Table
of the Elements

1 Poison						

1 Poison

3 Poison	4 Poison

11 Poison	12 Poison

2 Poison

5 Poison	6 Poison	7 Poison	8 Poison	9 Poison	10 Poison
13 Poison	14 Poison	15 Poison	16 Poison	17 Poison	18 Poison

Samuel

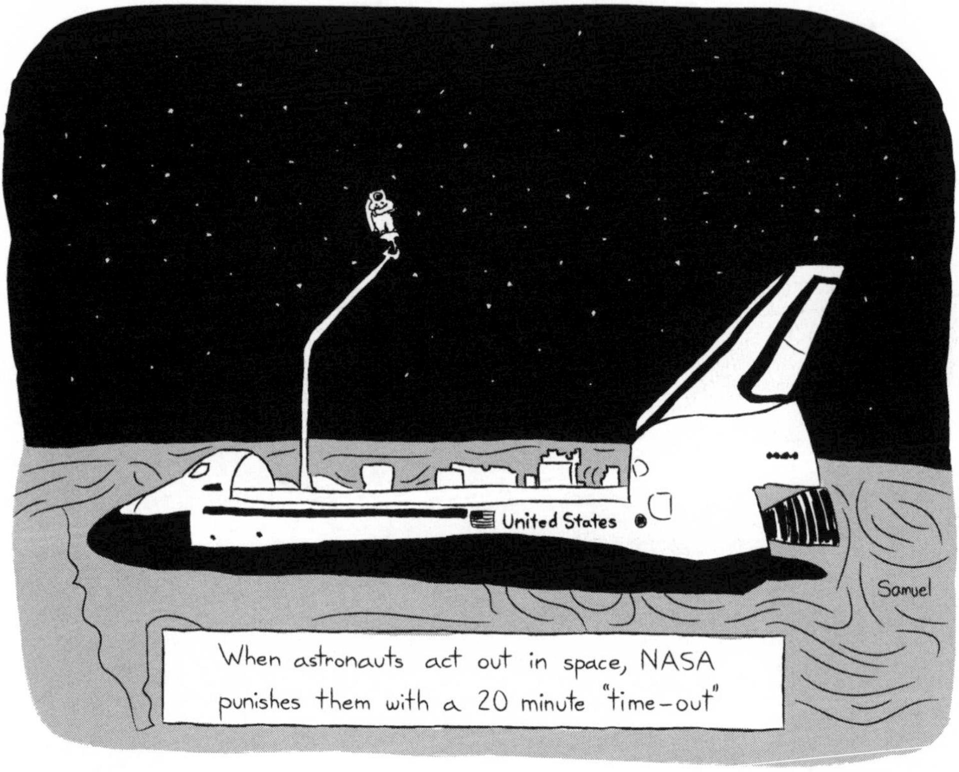
United States
Samuel
When astronauts act out in space, NASA punishes them with a 20 minute "time-out"

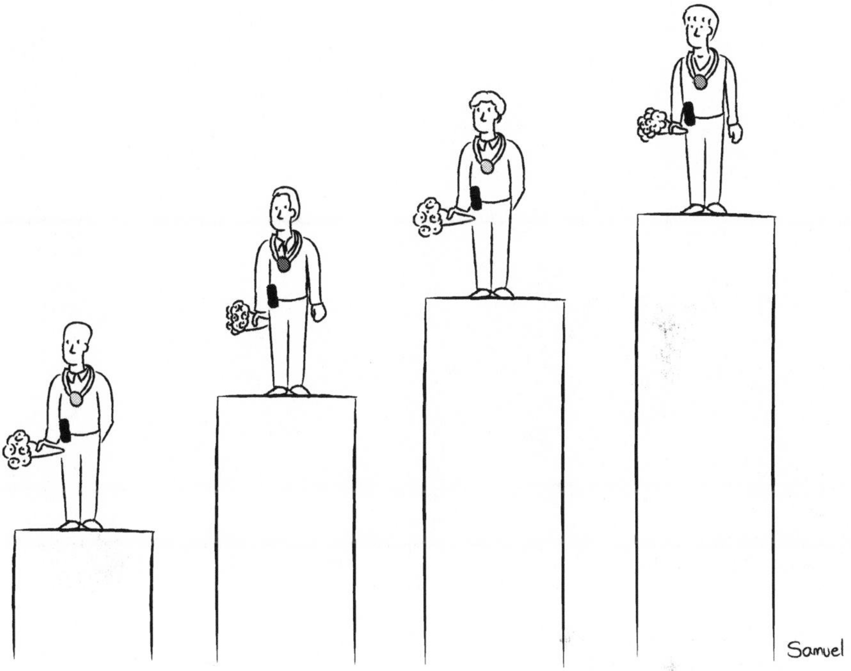
Samuel

Medal ceremony for best phone reception

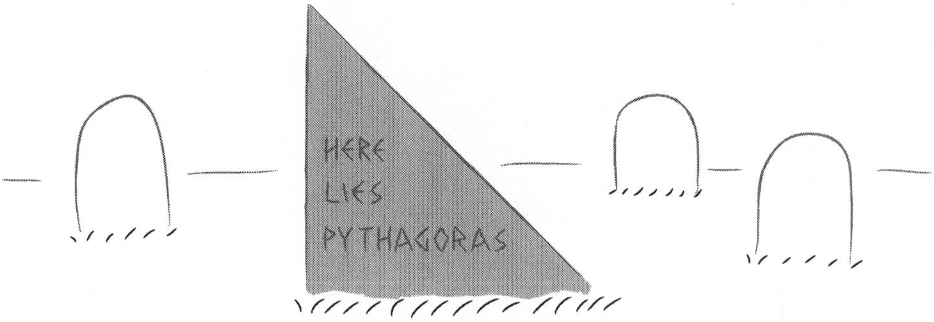
HERE
LIES
PYTHAGORAS

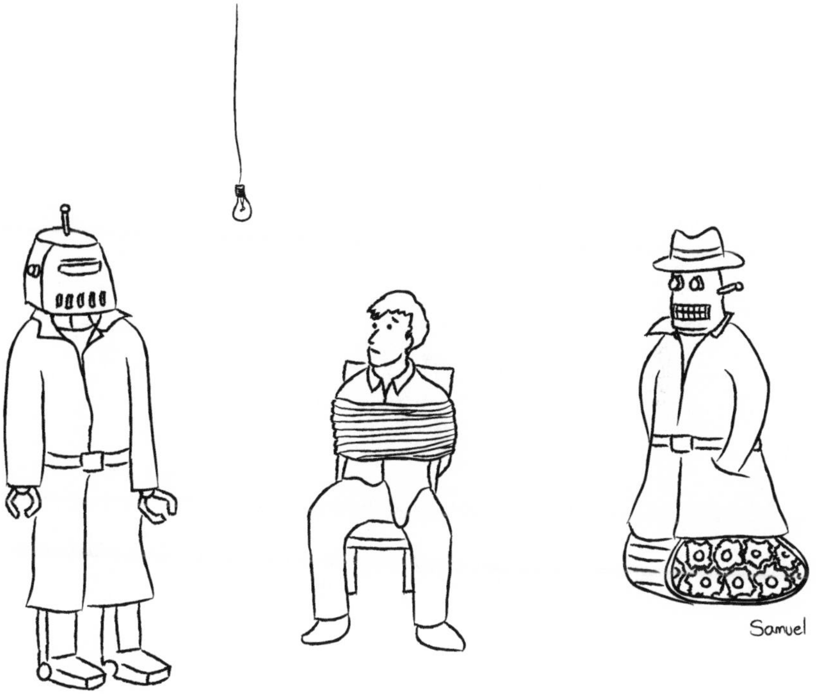
Samuel

"Talk or we release your internet history."

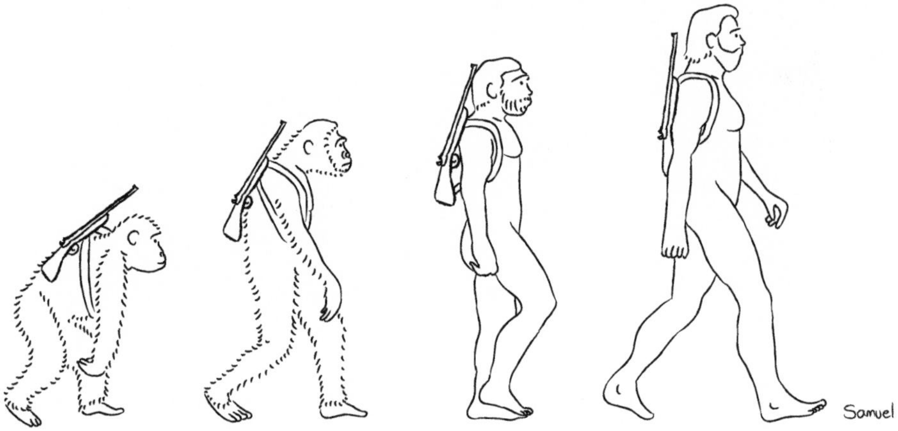
Samuel

Bipartisan compromise on teaching evolution

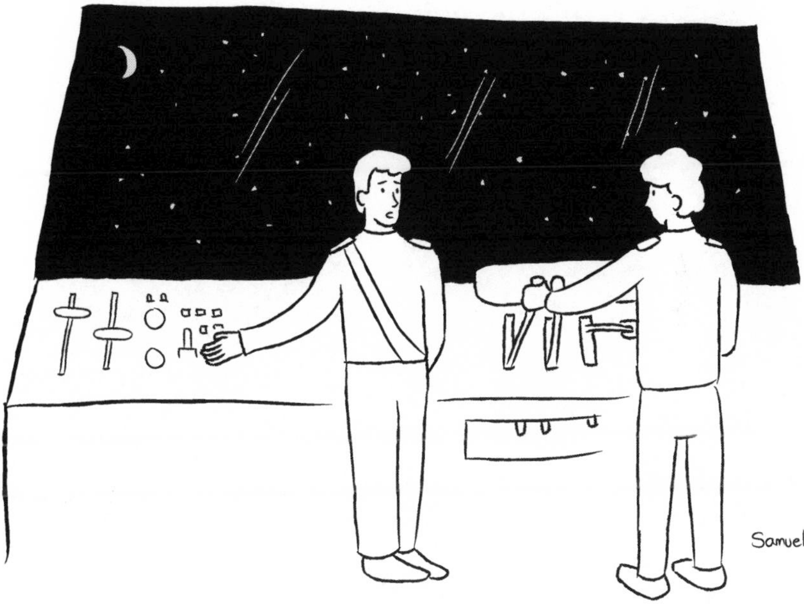
Samuel

"Here's the control panel. That's where we make lattés."

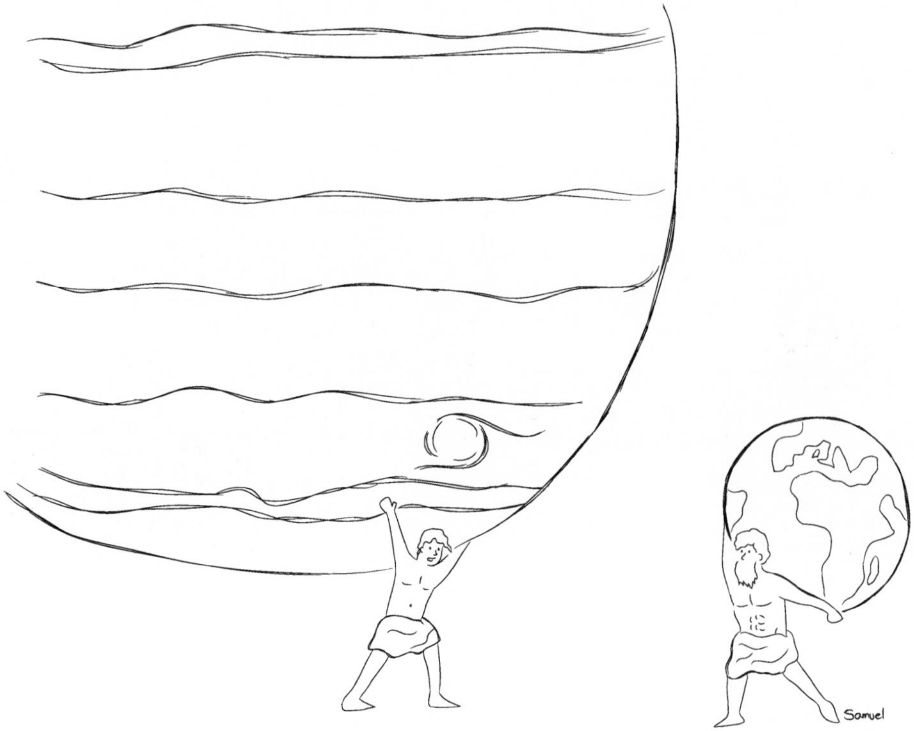
Samuel

"It's just gas."

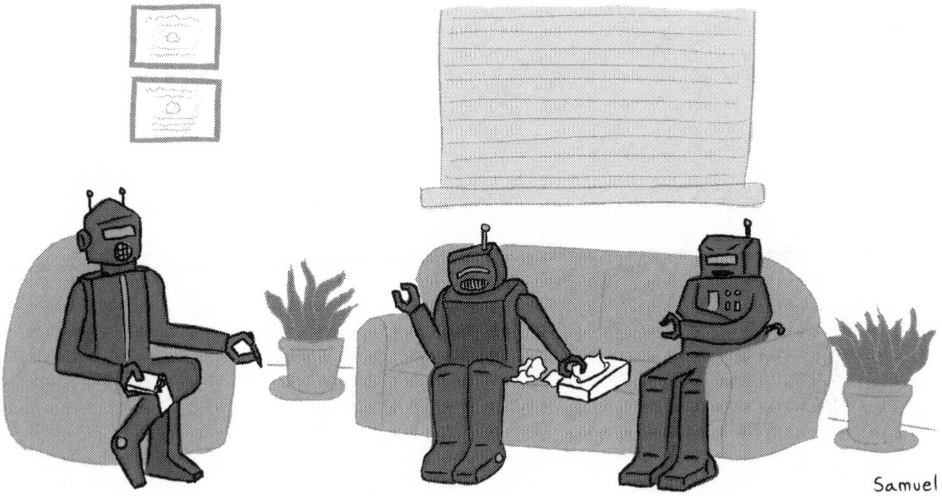
Samuel

"Sometimes, I just pretend to be out of batteries."

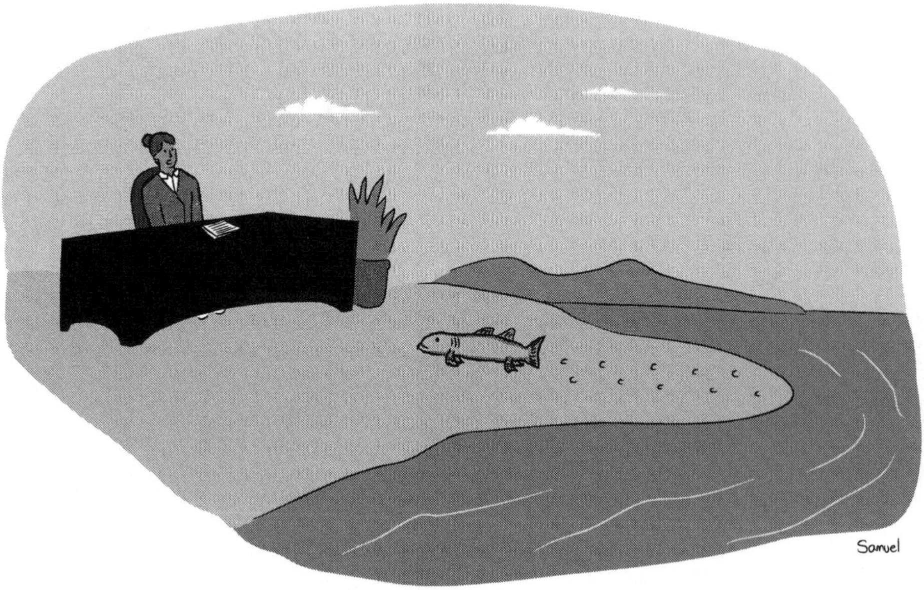
Samuel

"Where do you see yourself in five hundred million years?"

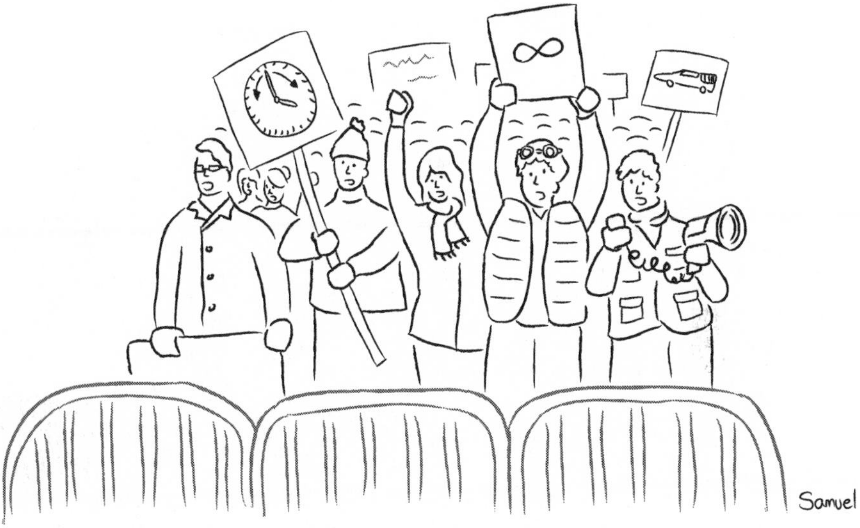
Samuel

"What do we want?"

"Time travel!"

"When do we want it?"

"Irrelevant!"

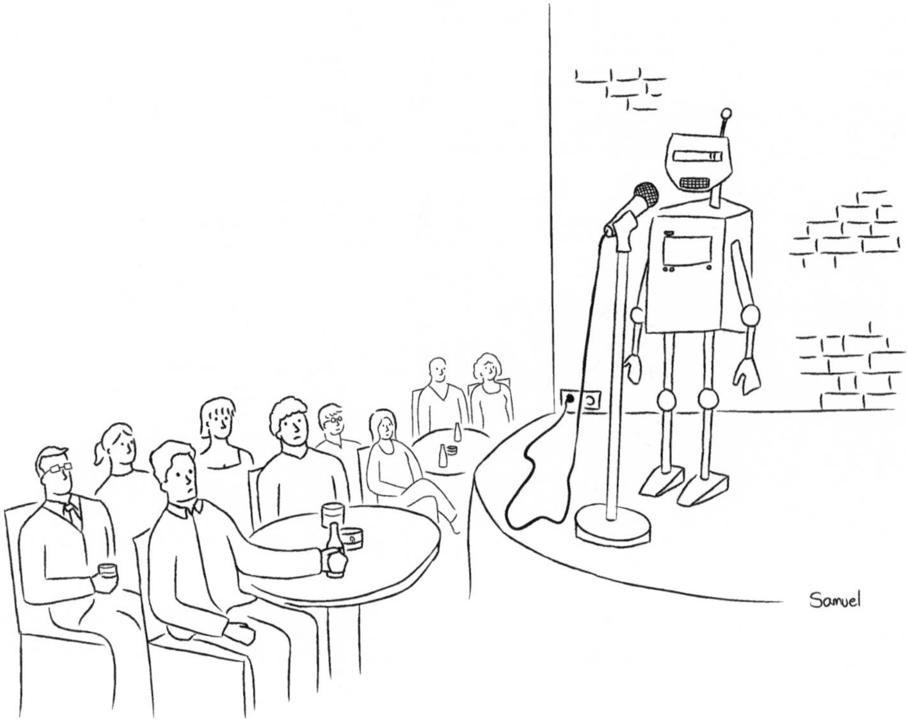
Samuel

"So, I'm singular."

Society

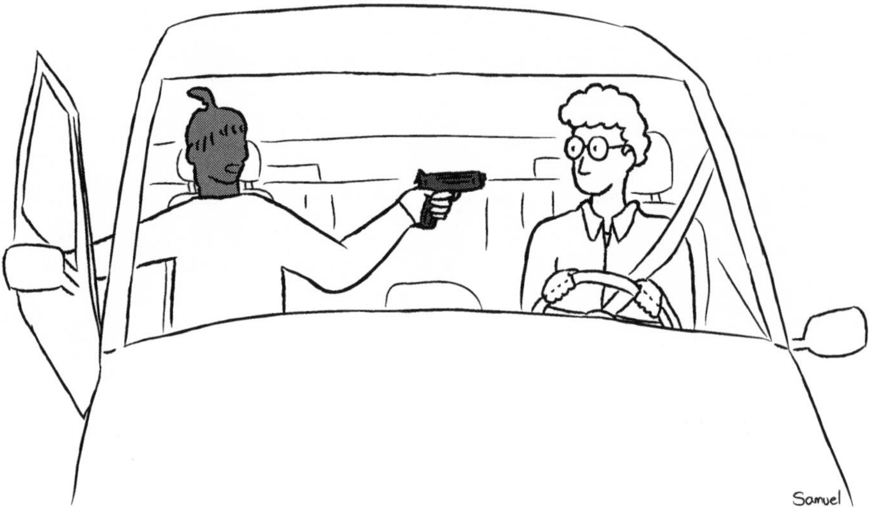
Samuel

"Think of this as a forced rideshare."

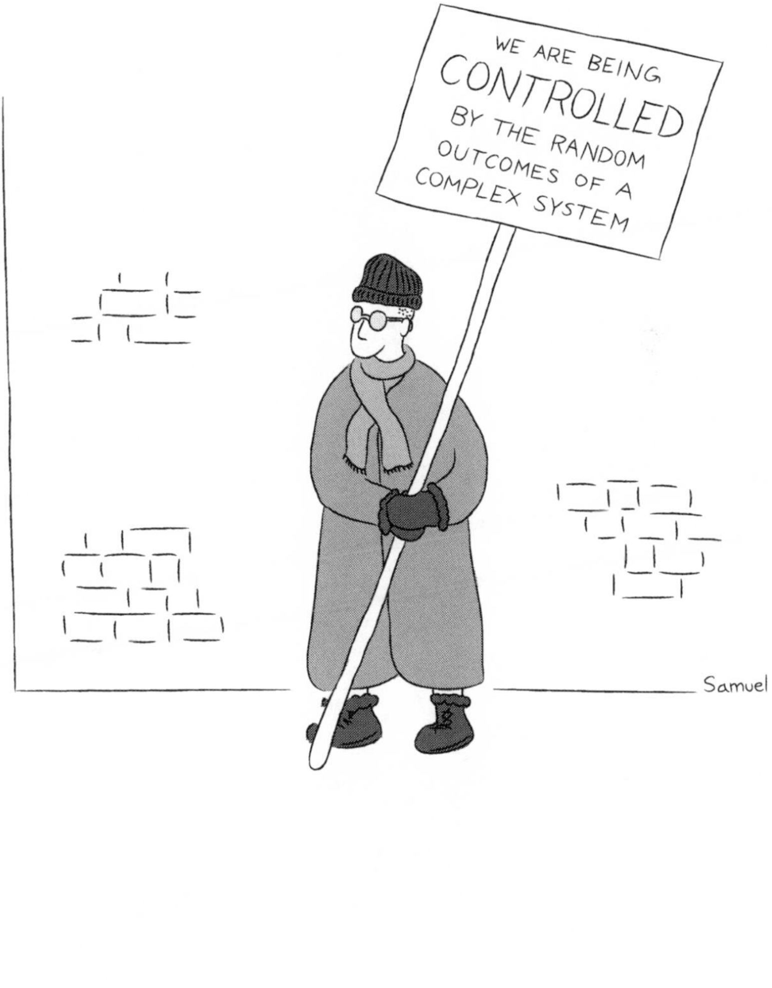
WE ARE BEING
CONTROLLED
BY THE RANDOM
OUTCOMES OF A
COMPLEX SYSTEM
Samuel

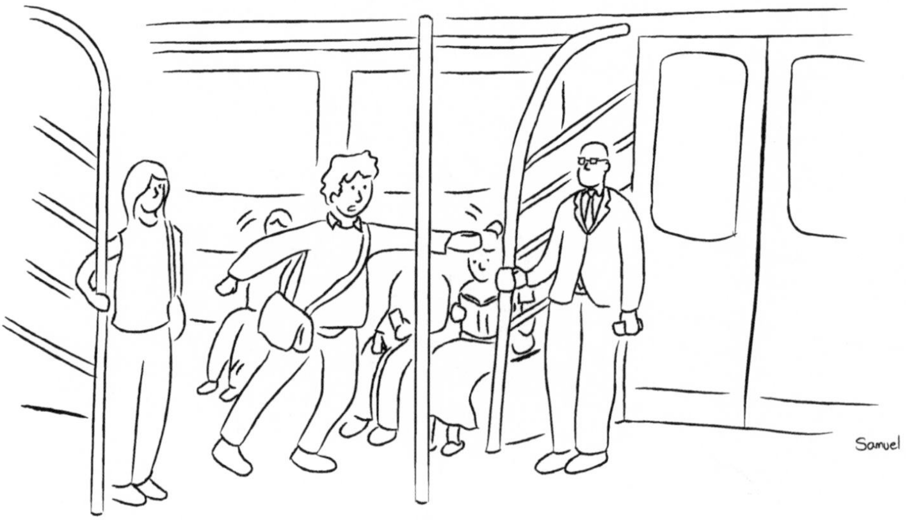
Samuel

"Sorry, I haven't yet found my subway legs."

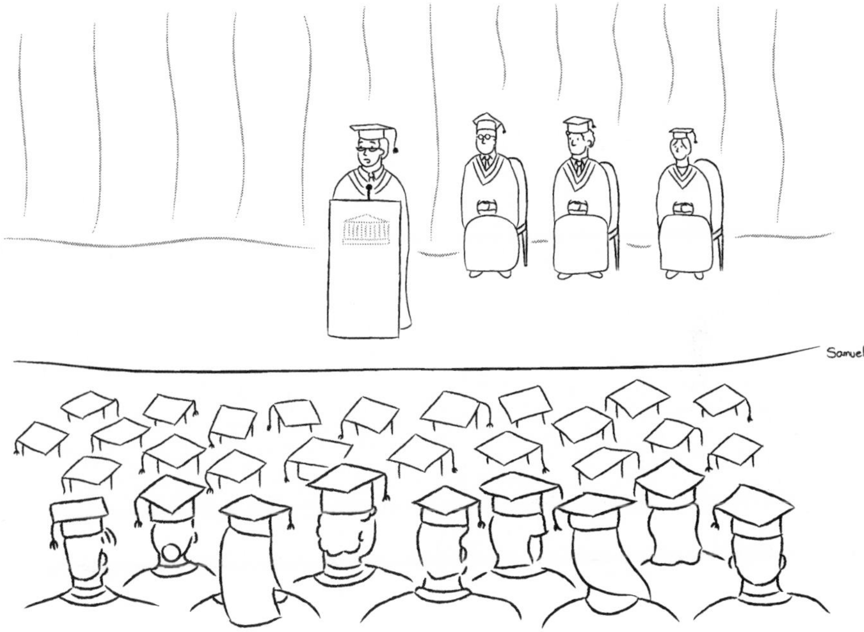
Samuel

"First, a disclaimer: the inspirational parts of this speech don't apply to liberal arts majors."

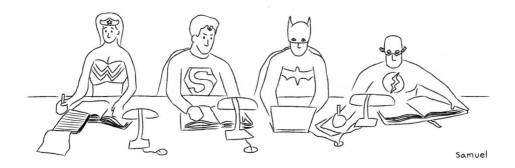

The Justice League reviews jurisprudence

Samuel

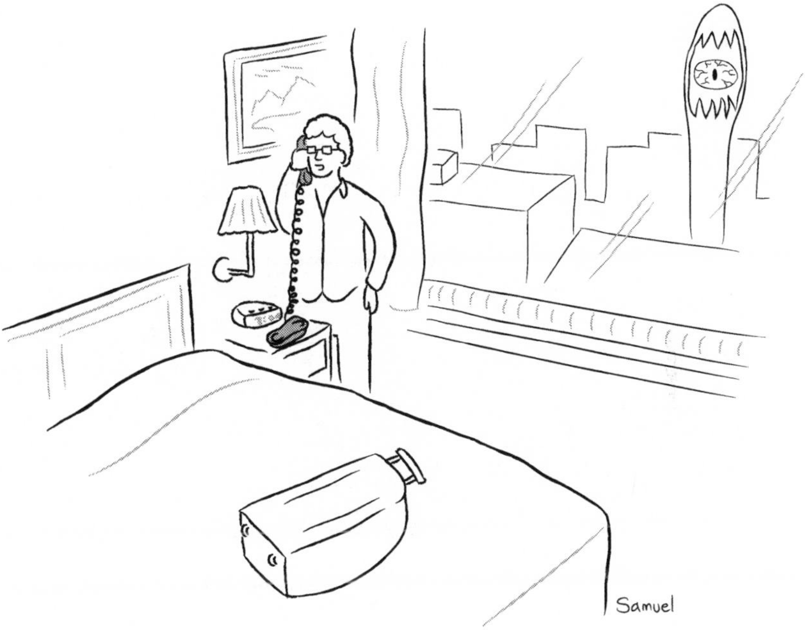
Samuel

"Could I possibly switch to a room that doesn't face the all-seeing eye?"

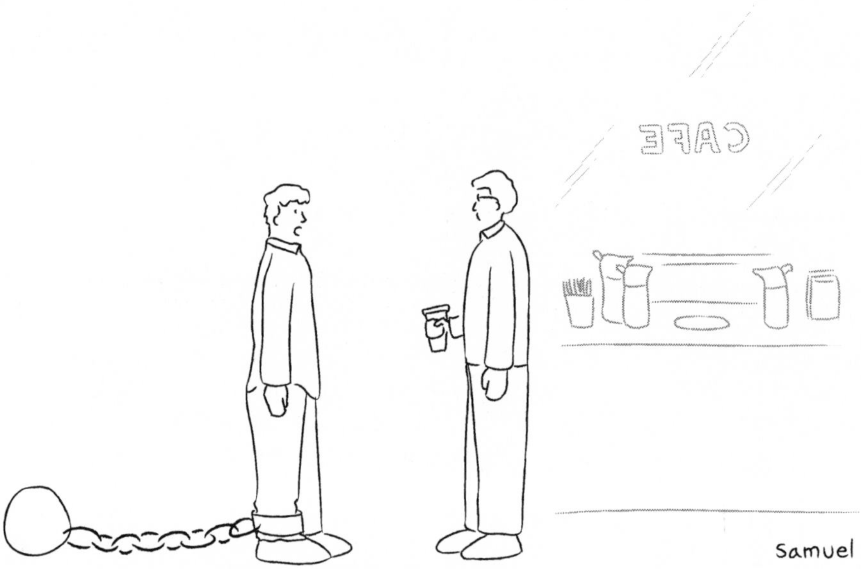
CAFE
samuel

"It's so I remember to bring back the bathroom key."

Politics

Samuel

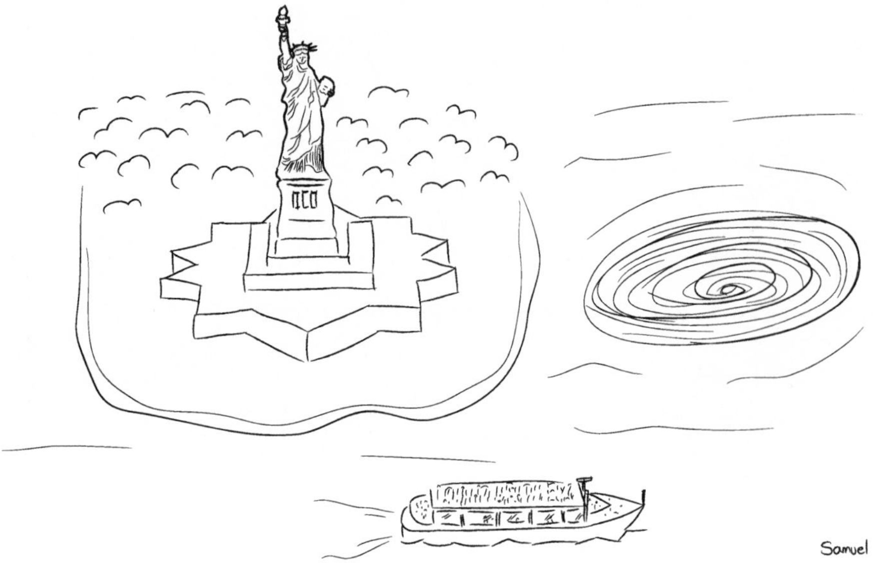
Samuel

"And just beside the Statue of Liberty
is the the Vortex of Student Debt."

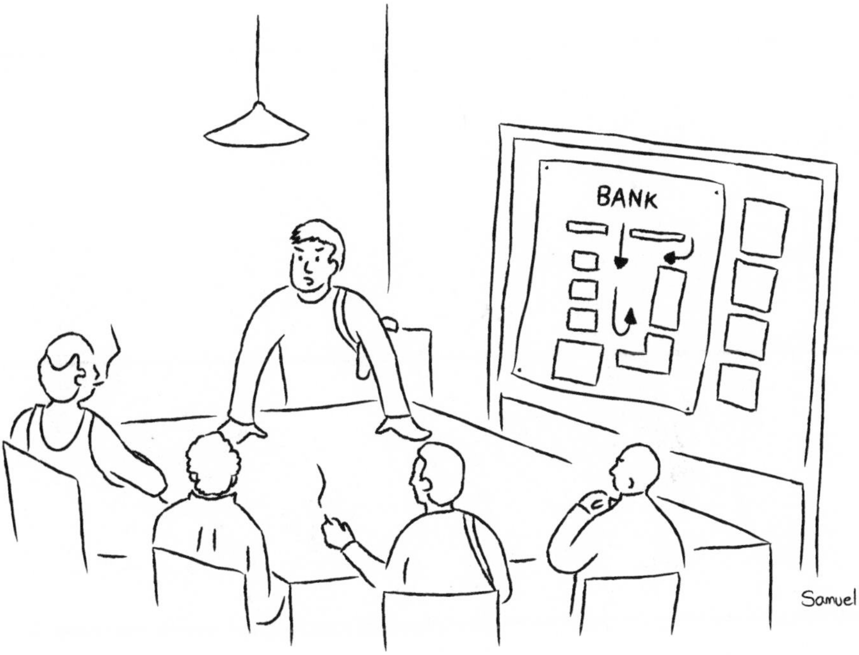
BANK
Samuel

"Here's the plan and don't worry; it's carbon neutral."

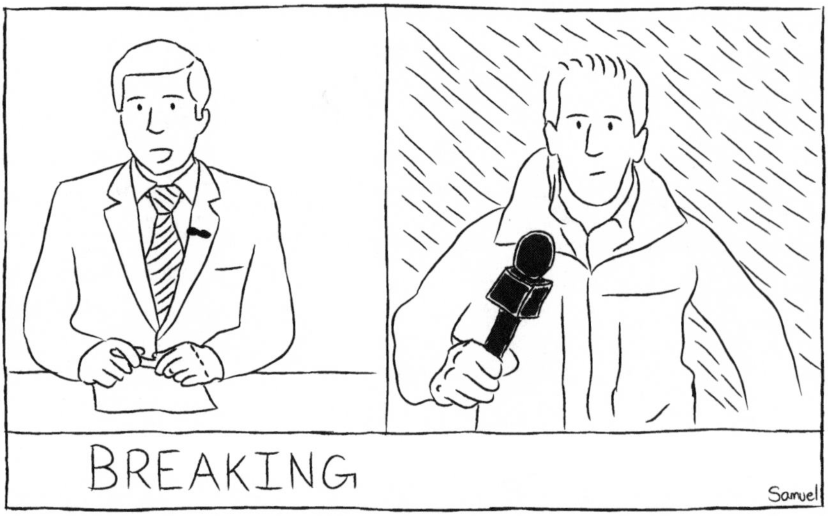
BREAKING
Samuel

"From where you are in the field, what kind of contrived, useless analysis can you give us?"

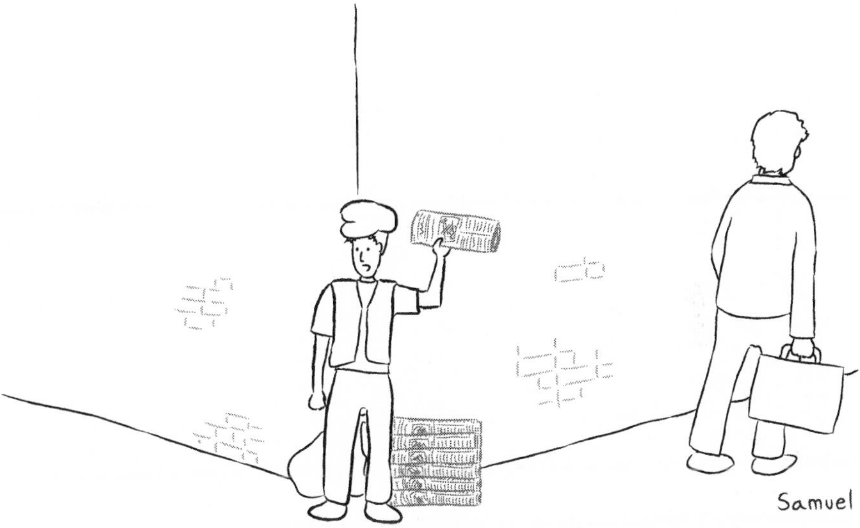
Samuel

"Extra! Extra! Glance at a headline and make a snap judgement."

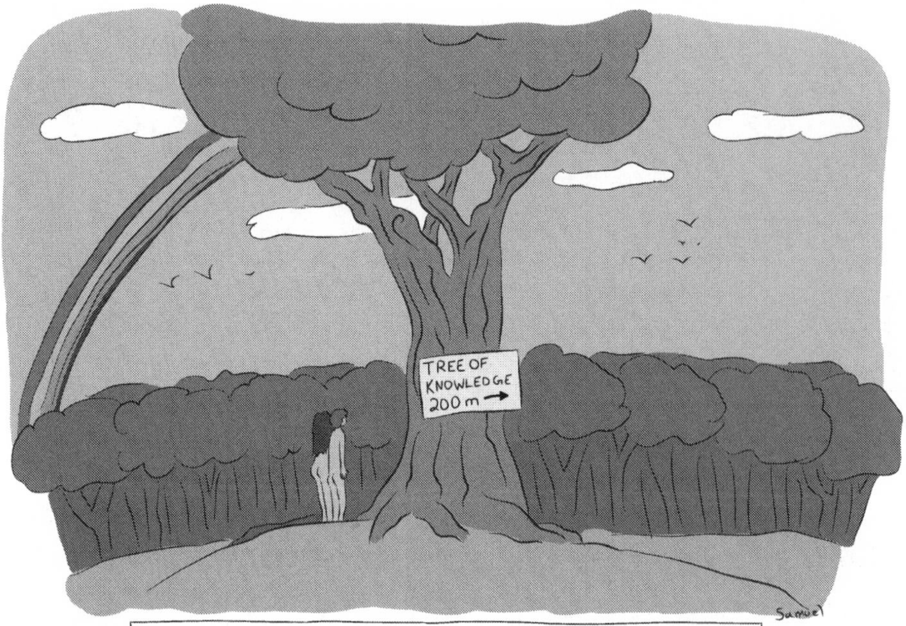
TREE OF
KNOWLEDGE
200 m →
Samuel

THE TREE OF EPISTEMOLOGY

Work

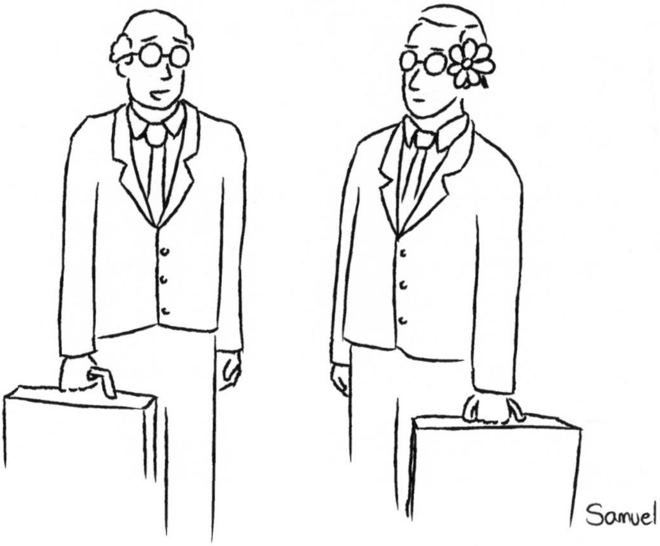
Samuel

"Since when are you such a free spirit?"

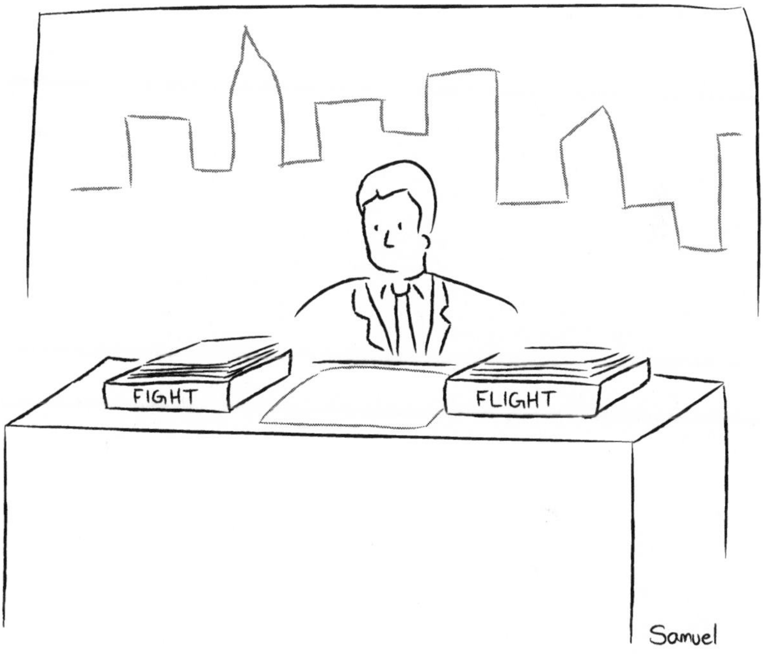
FIGHT
FLIGHT
Samuel

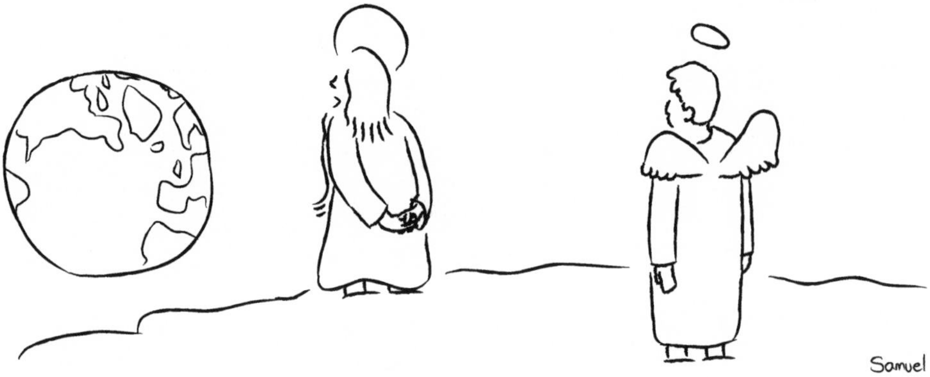
Samuel

"I'm most proud of my work as a job creator."

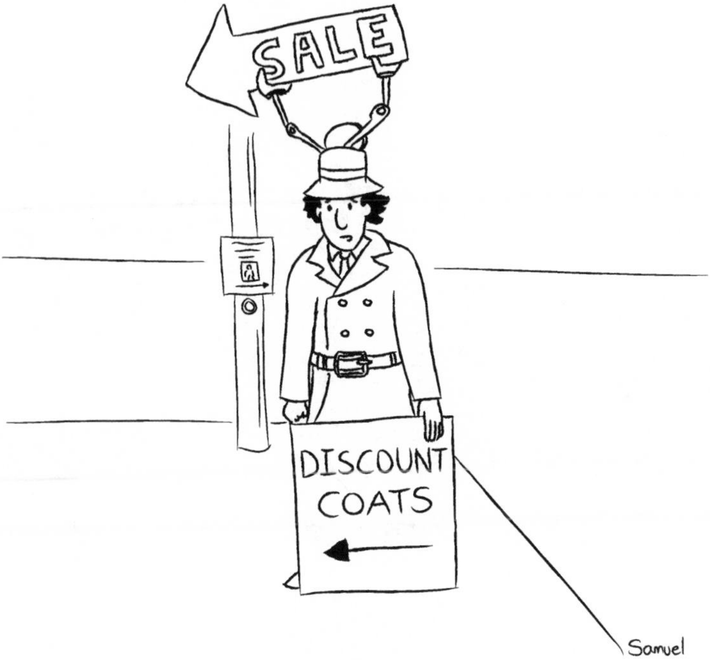
SALE
DISCOUNT COATS
Samuel

"Go go gadget dignity."

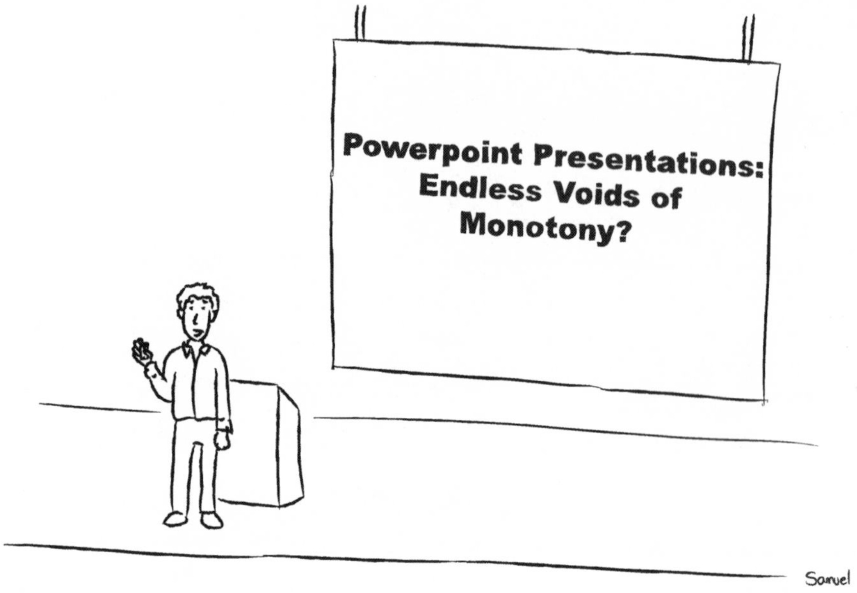
Powerpoint Presentations:
Endless Voids of
Monotony?
Samuel

"Next slide..."

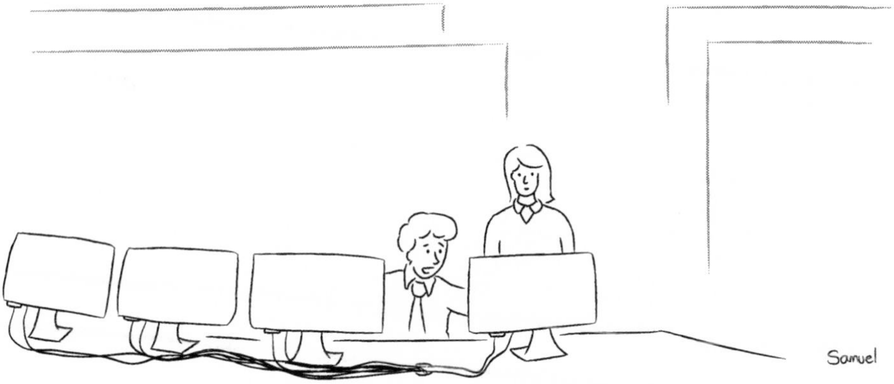
Samuel

"I use this one to keep track of what's happening on my other monitors."

Samuel

"Hey—you have to respect me,
I'm wearing a suit on a Saturday!"

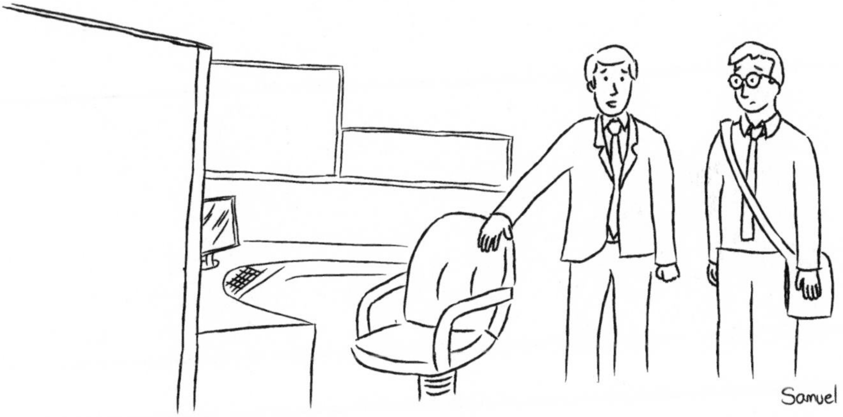
Samuel

"Here's where you'll spend the next five years slowly letting go of your dreams."

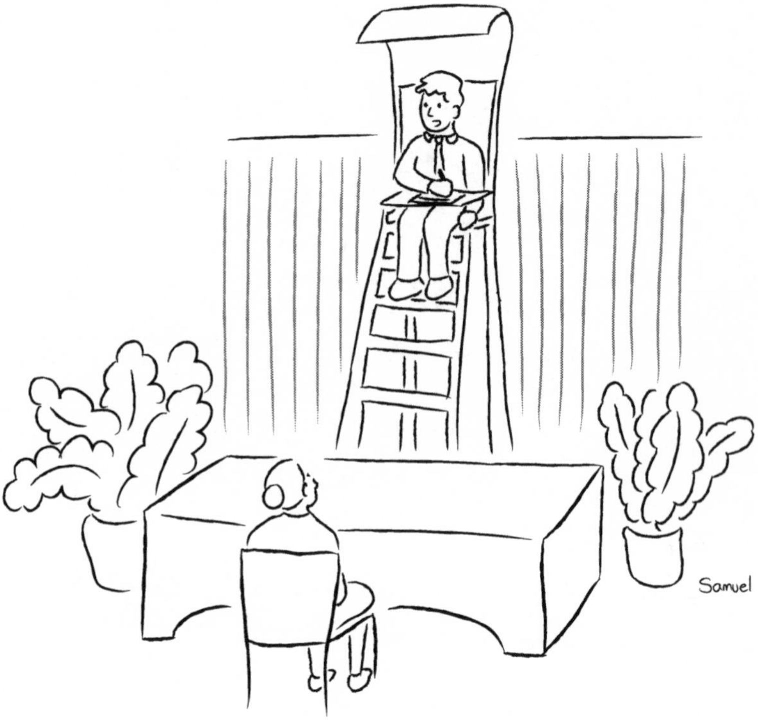
Samuel

"Why do you think you're qualified to officiate tennis?"

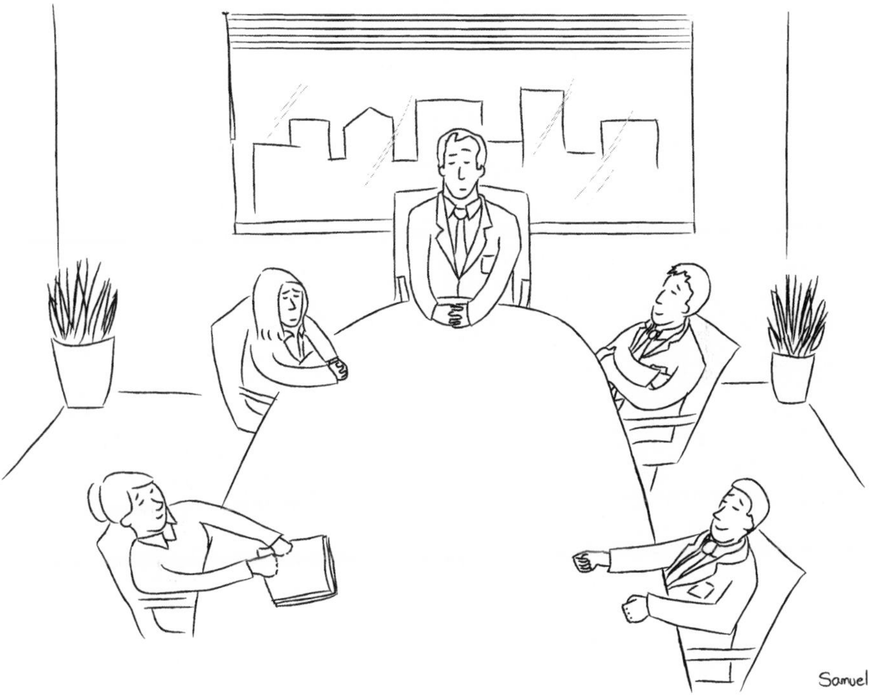
Samuel

Team-building kegel exercises

Samuel

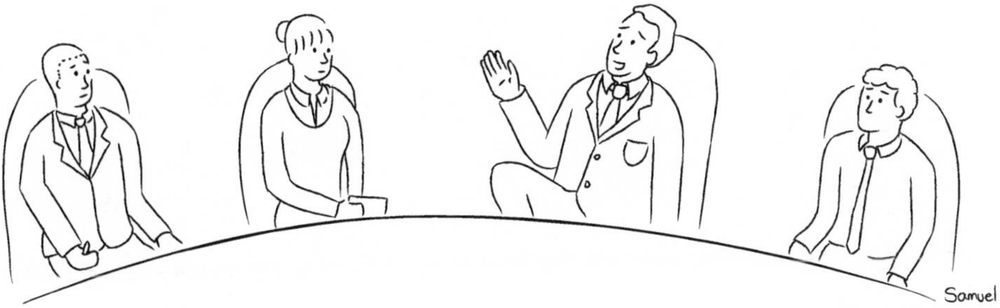
Samuel

"I just want to speak for a quick five that will evolve into a monotonous sixty."

Samuel

"Don't think of me as a boss. Think of me as a friend who is overbearing and short-tempered."

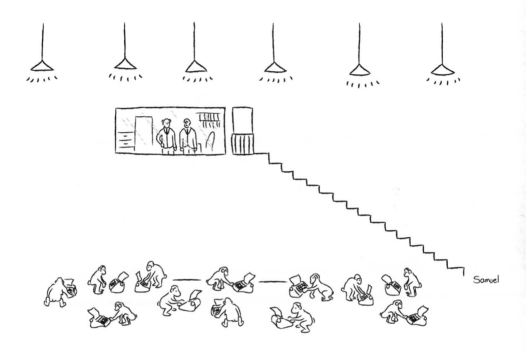

"A thousand monkeys on a thousand typewriters and all we have to show for it is a best-selling erotic novel."

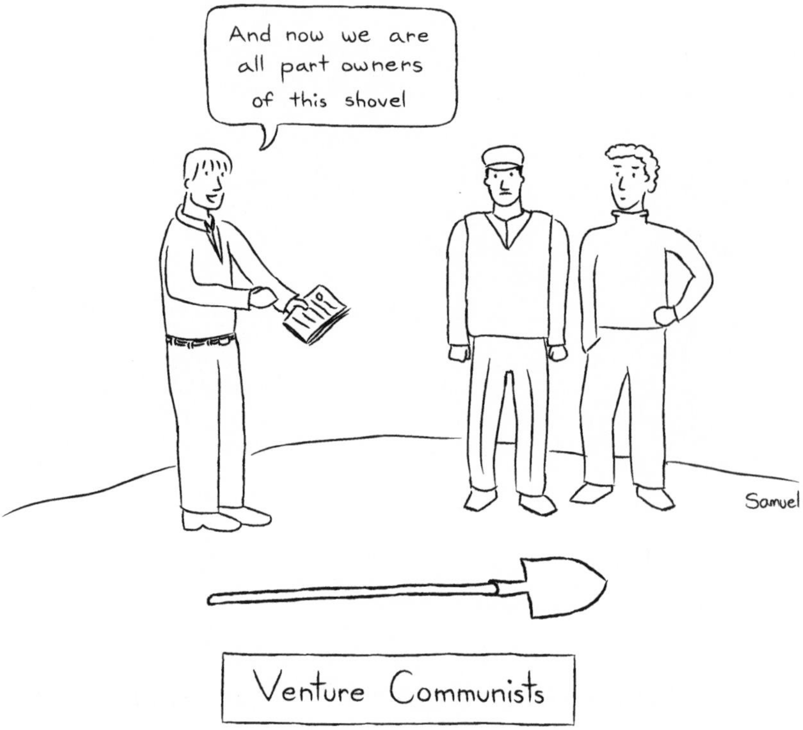
And now we are all part owners of this shovel
Samuel
Venture Communists

Samuel

"I'm not un-firing you just because of your fantastic jazz hands."

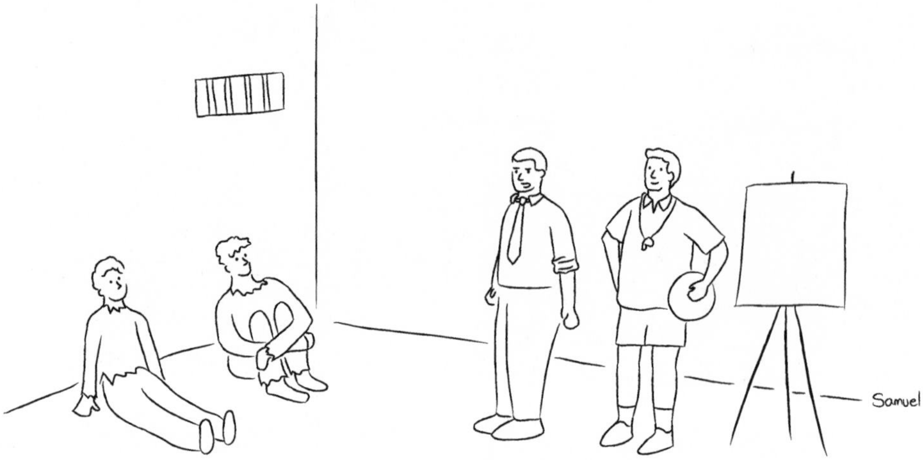
Samuel

"To crush your will to resist,
we're gonna do team-building exercises."

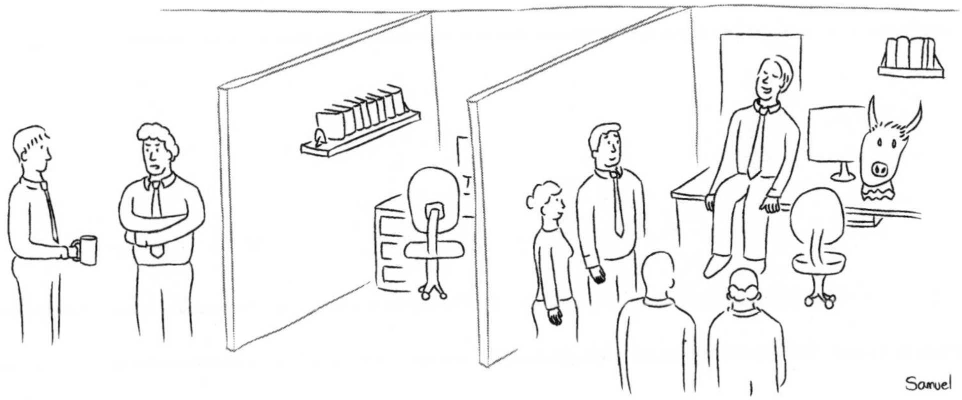
Samuel

"And now everyone thinks Greg is so great just because he slew the office minotaur."

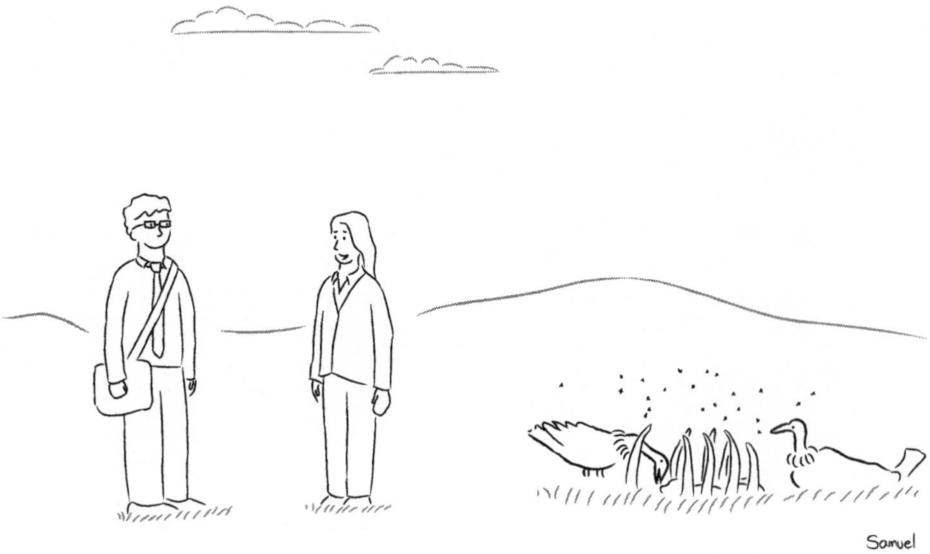
Samuel

"Our office is very open concept."

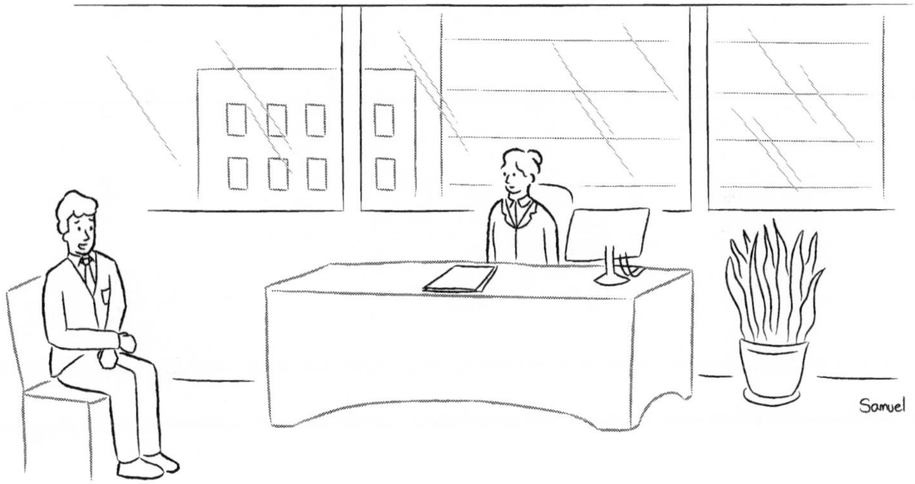
Samuel

"My greatest weakness is probably that I hate working."

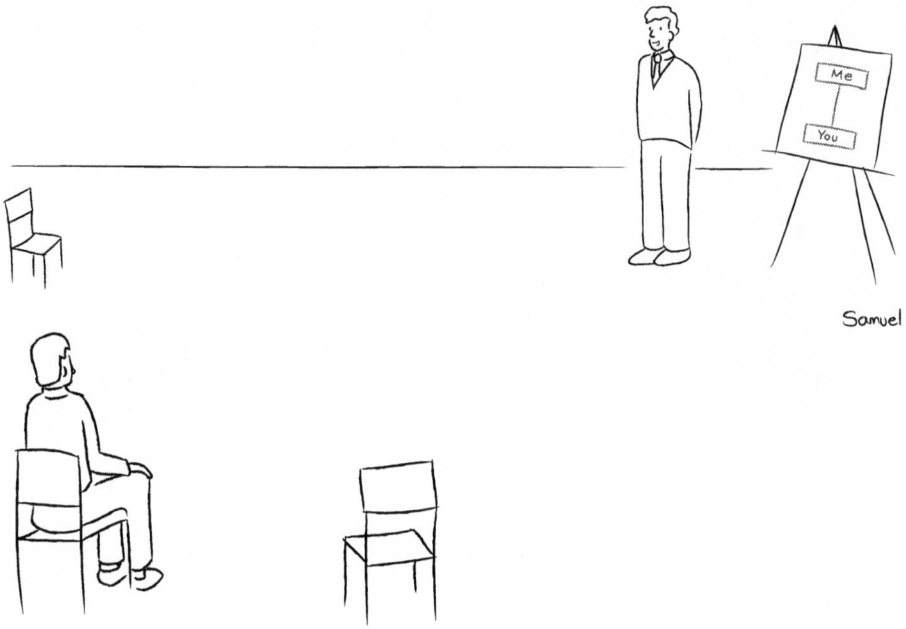
Me
You
Samuel

"Let's review the org chart."

CASUAL SEX FRIDAYS

Samuel

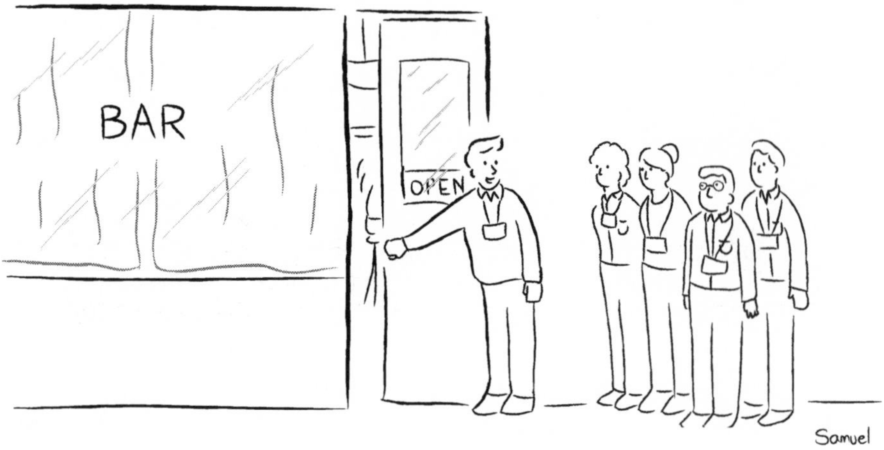
BAR
OPEN
Samuel

"Now it's time for the team-destroying exercises."

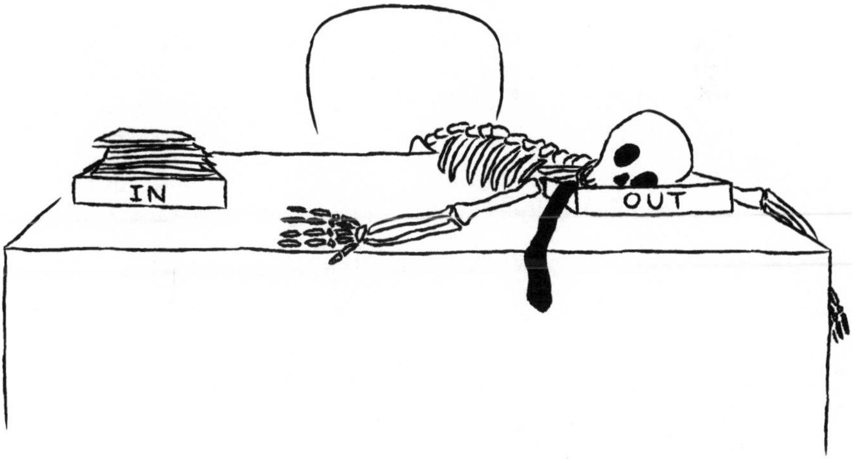
IN
OUT

Samuel

Jacob Samuel is an internationally-published humour cartoonist whose work has been featured in publications such as *The New Yorker*, *Harvard Business Review*, *Barron's*, *Geist*, *The Feathertale Review*, *Prospect*, *Wirtschaftswoche*, and on *CBC: Comedy*. He is also a stand-up comic who has performed on national TV and radio in Canada. Many of the cartoons in this book come from his webcomic, *The Daily Snooze*. For more: *mostresponsibleperson.org*.